The Architecture of Privacy

Courtney Bowman, Ari Gesher,
John K. Grant, and Daniel Slate

Edited by Elissa Lerner

Beijing · Boston · Farnham · Sebastopol · Tokyo

The Architecture of Privacy

by Courtney Bowman, Ari Gesher, John K. Grant, and Daniel Slate

Printed in the United States of America.

Published by O'Reilly Media, Inc., 1005 Gravenstein Highway North, Sebastopol, CA 95472.

O'Reilly books may be purchased for educational, business, or sales promotional use. Online editions are also available for most titles (*http://safaribooksonline.com*). For more information, contact our corporate/institutional sales department: 800-998-9938 or *corporate@oreilly.com*.

Editors: Elissa Lerner, Heather Scherer, and Mike Loukides	**Indexer:** WordCo Indexing Services
Production Editor: Colleen Lobner	**Interior Designer:** David Futato
Copyeditor: Christina Edwards	**Cover Designer:** Ellie Volckhausen
Proofreader: Gillian McGarvey	**Illustrator:** Rebecca Demarest

September 2015:   First Edition

Revision History for the First Edition
2015-08-26:   First Release

See *http://oreilly.com/catalog/errata.csp?isbn=9781491904015* for release details.

978-1-491-90401-5

[LSI]

Table of Contents

Part I. Getting Started

Part III. Oversight: Holding Users and Systems Accountable

Foreword

When I was an undergraduate majoring in computer science a few decades ago, books published by O'Reilly and Associates possessed talismanic power to me. As it happened, some of the earliest O'Reilly books were being published during my freshman year, and their mix of great writing, beautiful production value, and hyperspecificity were tailor-made for a young geek learning about Unix, perl, and the Internet for the first time. My dorm room bookshelves were lined with a rainbow of brightly colored book spines. Across my desk roamed a veritable menagerie of cover illustrations, from camels to grasshoppers, from crabs to crowned pigeons. I read every line of Dale Dougherty's book, and Cricket Liu's book; the tattered pages of my copy of Larry Wall's *Perl Programming* began to fall apart in my hands. I even splurged (well, my parents did) and bought the entire set of pricey X Window System guides, although I confess that I didn't read most of those.

I tell you this history to come clean: I gladly would've written a Foreword to contribute text to an O'Reilly book to honor my twenty-year-old self's obsession even if that book was just average. What a happy moment it is for me, then, to be able to contribute front matter to an O'Reilly book that is much more than just average. You hold in your hands (or view on your screen) a fantastic contribution to the burgeoning literature of privacy engineering.

Privacy requires a dialogue between two types of people: those who speak policy and those who speak engineering. The most important word of that sentence—and the part that many people fail to understand—is "dialogue." In many other spaces where tech touches policy, these two tribes stand across a chasm, reacting *to* one another but not conversing *with* one another. Thus, in modern digital copyright policy, creators create, technologists protect and circumvent, and lawyers create laws and spur lawsuits reacting to these actions. In telecommunications policy, engineers engineer and lawyers react and respond.

And even in a field that many people—including many experts—mistakenly think relates closely to privacy—information security—the dialogue is hardly essential.

Security folks traffic in the impossible and possible—this crypto works or it is broken. The benchmarks for "victory" and "defeat" are entirely internal to the discipline. And the law and policy folks sit on the sidelines and react and respond.

Privacy doesn't work this way. A privacy engineer, at least a good one, cannot live in ignorance of law and policy because the ideas of "victory" and "defeat" for privacy cannot be subjected to correctness proofs and measurements of algorithmic complexity. Engineers can tell you how to dial down or dial up a particular information flow, but it requires a source external and foreign to the engineer's core training—maybe the law department, public relations, the shareholders, or the engineer's moral compass—to determine right and wrong, acceptable risk or not, privacy violation or not.

As only one example, take the topics of data anonymization and re-identification, topics central to work I have done. This much we now know: "data can either be useful or perfectly anonymous but never both." I said this once, and much ink has been spilled trying to prove me wrong. I'm not wrong, but at the same time, I am not being very interesting when I say it. Of course scrubbed data can be unscrubbed. You would be foolish indeed (or worse, trying to sell anonymization consulting services) to fail to realize that modern improvements in data processing, auxiliary data, and storage could lead to any other result. But recognizing this boring truth is far from knowing what to do about it. The lesson of powerful re-identification isn't that we take our ball and go home. But it is just as unacceptable to continue to act as nothing has changed.

You cannot "solve" the re-identification problem without lawyers who understand tech and techies who understand policy. (I try to be both, as I went to law school a few years after obtaining that CS degree and now teach law.) It might be enough to delete eighteen identifiers or it might not. It might be enough to encrypt the data and leave the key with "Joan in the front office," or it might not. Maybe you can distribute the data to a trusted third party, or maybe you shouldn't. It's nuance and hard choices and a dialogue between engineers and lawyers all the way down. We need to train a new breed of privacy engineer, and it starts with creating a literature elaborating this new discipline.

This bringing together of engineering and law means that it takes an exceptional group of people to come together to write a proper book on this topic. Luckily for you, and for the privacy community as a whole, the authors of this book compose such a group. They include top-notch engineers and good lawyers. But more importantly, they include people steeped in the weird mental gymnastics, arcane training, and time spent in rooms in Silicon Valley and state and national capitals required to be called privacy experts.

It is even luckier for you that they happen also to be extremely engaging writers. This is a very well-produced and organized book. It has the virtues of clarity and modesty, two virtues often lacking in books written by engineers. I call the book modest, because it recognizes that this field is new and that we don't really even yet understand what we mean when we call somebody a privacy engineer.

I'm not sure I'm ready to call this book a classic or a new entrant into the canon. I think time will tell, and I hope I am invited back to update this Foreword for the second edition, when I can trot out those labels, if they stick. But this seems to me at least to be a very useful book, one that fills a gaping hole in the current literature. I'll happily place my copy of this book on my shelf. I have a particular spot in mind where I think it will fit in well.

—Paul Ohm
Professor of Law,
Georgetown University Law Center
Boulder, Colorado
July 2015

Preface

Who Should Read This Book

This book is not for privacy experts.

If you are looking for an in-depth discussion of the legal implications of the *Kyllo v. United States (2001)* Supreme Court decision or thorough exploration of how to implement differential privacy in a database, then you should look elsewhere. There is no shortage of invaluable literature on these and many other privacy-related topics, and we recommend it to those readers.

This book is for privacy beginners. Those who have a niggling worry that the technology they are creating raises privacy concerns and want to do something about it, but who also are not going to spend the next 10 years perusing privacy case law and academic papers trying to figure out how to port those lessons into lines of code.

It's also for those who have a basic understanding of law and privacy policy, but who cannot read lines of code to save their lives. It's OK—you don't need to be an engineer to read this book. And even after you read it from cover to cover, you still won't be able to write code for access controls. But you will have an understanding of the range of possibilities when it comes to basic privacy-protective technical capabilities. You'll know what to ask your coders to build.

You may be surprised how frequently what you build has privacy implications, but we live in a time of increasing capabilities for personal re-identification. This book will help you be familiar with how to spot privacy questions. If you read nothing else but Chapter 1, you'll understand better how to judge whether or not what you're doing is connected to data privacy.

Whether you're building a new smartphone app in your dorm room or a database empire from your garage, *The Architecture of Privacy* will be your first step into the world of privacy engineering.

Why We Wrote This Book

Decisions made by engineers can unleash technology upon the world that can significantly affect fundamental rights. In some cases, this can yield positive outcomes such as the creation of new platforms to exchange ideas that catalyze change in the world's most oppressive regimes. In other cases, new technologies can become tools of repression and control, enabling governments and corporate interests to track and manipulate individuals with surprising subtlety and at remarkable scale. With such high stakes, it must be in the interest of more than just lawyers and bureaucrats to recognize, promote, or guard against these potential outcomes as needed.

This book is, in part, an effort to empower the engineer. Successful technology is not just technology that works; it is technology that works while simultaneously offering capabilities that protect privacy and civil liberties. Readers of this book will not have to watch helplessly as their technology is misused, nor will they have to wait for others to try to curb that misuse. Instead, they will have the tools to recognize potential risks and design against them, sparing much headache and heartache.

This book is distinctive in the realm of privacy literature as it is written by technical authors who approach privacy and civil liberties from what is currently a highly atypical perspective: how to engineer technologies that will deliver trustworthy safeguards capable of supporting liberal-democratic principles. By contrast, most privacy books are written by professional scholars who take law and policy as their starting point and treat technological concerns as ancillary at best and menacing at worst, which is hardly a perspective that will encourage the engineers of the world.

But this book is not just for engineers. For the non-engineers who read this book—the academics, lawyers, and policymakers—we offer a new perspective. The policy choice is not simply to build or not to build, to ban or not to ban. Instead, these readers will find that engineers can offer an arsenal of technical tools that can form the building blocks of nuanced policies that maximize both privacy protection *and* utility. This book provides a menu of what to demand in a new technology.

A Word on Privacy and Technology Today

Over the past few years, the public has become aware of the vast scale of data collected and held by governments and corporations. As we produce more data about ourselves through the ubiquitous use of electronic payment systems, mobile devices, and cloud computing services, the institutions around us have concluded that this data holds tremendous value. Unfortunately, the private companies and government agencies that hold data about us do not always put appropriate safeguards in place to prevent deliberate or accidental privacy violations. Sometimes this is because of gaps in their internal policies, or because they misjudged risk or their ability to mitigate it. But sometimes it's because these organizations don't have data management systems that offer the technical capabilities necessary to support robust, privacy-protective policies.

That need not be the case. Today we know enough to design systems that build in, from the beginning, appropriate safeguards that can substantially reduce the chances of abuse or mistakes when handling people's sensitive data. We believe it is time to move away from all systems that don't have these straightforward and sensible protections in place. We have become heavily reliant on advanced information technology, and we need to be able to trust our systems and each other with our data.

Effective privacy-facilitating technology is designed to minimize the friction between a person and their work. Capabilities can and should be designed in such a way that they enable privacy-protective policies and procedures while creating as few hurdles as possible in using the system. The easier privacy protections are to use and the more unnoticeable they are to everyday users, the more likely these protections will be embraced. As soon as a privacy-protective feature becomes cumbersome, some users will look for ways to avoid it or develop shortcuts that will undermine its overall effectiveness. We advocate reducing potential friction by adhering to what is sometimes referred to as "privacy by design"—an approach that incorporates thinking about privacy-protective features and implementing them as early as possible. Capabilities that are part of the core functionality of the product are far less likely to cause friction than those simply grafted on to the technology late in the development process. Specific advice on how to incorporate privacy by design into your product can be found in extensive documentation on the topic elsewhere (*http://privacybyde sign.ca/*).

It is important to note that nothing described in this book could be said to *automatically* protect privacy. Simply having these capabilities in your system won't guarantee that privacy is protected. Rather, these capabilities must work in concert with legal frameworks and policy in order to be effective. Privacy law is an extremely nuanced field that often depends on subjective evaluations of the legitimacy of certain actions (and those evaluations can change rapidly depending on outside factors)—something that is very difficult to hardcode into a technology.

Access controls, for example (see Part II), are a powerful tool for managing data use, but a user must configure those controls in order to ensure that data is accessed by those who have the authority to see it, and denied to those who do not. Meanwhile, the mere existence of audit logs (see Part III) is not enough to ensure rigorous oversight of system usage—someone must actually read those logs and take effective action when they see misuse of the data. Though just about anything is possible in the world of technology, we should maintain healthy skepticism of any technology that claims to automatically protect privacy while maximizing data utility.

Most likely, any attempt to automate privacy protection is going to lead to a system that is either unnecessarily restrictive, thereby undermining the utility of the system, or too permissive, thereby leaving ample room for misuse of the data (which might not be caught because oversight is reduced on the erroneous assumption that the system can govern itself).

Navigating This Book

We have tried to write this book in a way that allows readers to skip around, focusing on the topics most relevant to their needs. But we've also tried to ensure that the book hangs together as whole. Our narrative thread therefore goes something like this:

Whenever you collect and process personal and/or sensitive data, you have an obligation—moral in all cases, legal in most—to protect that data from theft, misuse, and abuse. You are directly responsible for designing and implementing security-enhancing and privacy-protective technologies and policies. This is hard! Understanding the different ways in which data can be personally identifying, recognizing the privacy risks associated with different technologies and use cases, implementing measures to mitigate those risks without compromising your original goals, and staying up-to-date on relevant law and policy are complex challenges, and there's no guaranteed recipe for success. There are, however, several broad categories of technology and policy that are foundational to protecting privacy and civil liberties, and you'll want to build on these strong foundations.

The opening four chapters of this book focus on the fundamental building blocks necessary to create a privacy-protective system. Chapter 1 is a brief history of the intersections of informational privacy, technology, and privacy law, which situates the reader in the context surrounding these issues. Chapters 2 and 3 cover the data collection technology, policy, and practices that should be transparent to your users or data subjects and should ensure that the kind and amount of data collected is proportional to your product's or service's stated purposes. Chapter 4 addresses high-level information security technology and policy needed to protect data from theft and other forms of *unauthorized access*.

Privacy technology and policy should ensure that data accessed through *authorized* means is protected from misuse and abuse. This goal is best achieved through some combination of access control and oversight measures.

Chapters 5, 6, and 7 address various ways of restricting and controlling authorized access to data. We describe how to grant differentiated access to the various levels of your system (e.g., application, network, hardware, etc.) and apply controls to varying levels of granularity in your data (e.g., system-level, record-level, cell-level, etc.). We describe different types of access (e.g., read, write, discovery, etc.) and conditions under which access is granted (selective-, purpose-, and scope-driven revelation). We describe federated system architectures that delegate some access-control decisions to the owners of systems separate from your own.

Chapters 8, 9, and 10 center on oversight, the necessary counterpart to access control. In order to hold the system and your users accountable, we present techniques for logging user activity in a way that makes data use auditable. We explain how data retention policies and data-purging technologies should be designed and implemented in a way that complies with regulations and minimizes privacy risks without compromising the usefulness of the system.

In Chapter 11, we walk through several case studies that demonstrate how these various building blocks can be assembled to solve real problems. In Chapter 12, we describe the role and responsibilities of the Privacy Engineer, an individual who will become increasingly critical to companies that process personal information. Finally, in Chapter 13, we share some thoughts on the future of privacy and how you can prepare for it.

In general, think of the capabilities described in the chapters that follow as a set of building blocks. They can be combined in a variety of ways to support different privacy imperatives. However, not all of these capabilities need to be used in every information system, and not all privacy issues that might arise from the use of those systems can be solved by these technologies.

Safari® Books Online

Safari Books Online is an on-demand digital library that delivers expert content in both book and video form from the world's leading authors in technology and business.

Technology professionals, software developers, web designers, and business and creative professionals use Safari Books Online as their primary resource for research, problem solving, learning, and certification training.

Safari Books Online offers a range of plans and pricing for enterprise, government, education, and individuals.

Members have access to thousands of books, training videos, and prepublication manuscripts in one fully searchable database from publishers like O'Reilly Media, Prentice Hall Professional, Addison-Wesley Professional, Microsoft Press, Sams, Que, Peachpit Press, Focal Press, Cisco Press, John Wiley & Sons, Syngress, Morgan Kaufmann, IBM Redbooks, Packt, Adobe Press, FT Press, Apress, Manning, New Riders, McGraw-Hill, Jones & Bartlett, Course Technology, and hundreds more. For more information about Safari Books Online, please visit us online.

How to Contact Us

Please address comments and questions concerning this book to the publisher:

O'Reilly Media, Inc.
1005 Gravenstein Highway North
Sebastopol, CA 95472
800-998-9938 (in the United States or Canada)
707-829-0515 (international or local)
707-829-0104 (fax)

We have a web page for this book, where we list errata, examples, and any additional information. You can access this page at *http://bit.ly/architecture-of-privacy*.

To comment or ask technical questions about this book, send email to *bookquestions@oreilly.com*.

For more information about our books, courses, conferences, and news, see our website at *http://www.oreilly.com*.

Find us on Facebook: *http://facebook.com/oreilly*

Follow us on Twitter: *http://twitter.com/oreillymedia*

Watch us on YouTube: *http://www.youtube.com/oreillymedia*

Acknowledgments

All the authors wish to acknowledge the extraordinary efforts of Elissa Lerner, editor of this book. Put simply, this book would not exist without her tireless efforts to herd this unruly band of cats as they blew through deadline after deadline and were readily distracted by new and exciting tangents.

We also wish to thank Palantir Technologies and its CEO, Dr. Alex Karp, for encouraging us in this effort. Although the book and its contents in no way represent the views of Palantir Technologies or any of its other employees, these authors would not have met and set out on this course without the support of the Palantir family and their tireless dedication to making the world a better place through technology.

We acknowledge a huge debt of gratitude to Dr. Lawrence Lessig, whose work in this space inspired both the title of this book and our whole approach to the interaction of legal and technical code. We also thank Paul Ohm for contributing an insightful Foreword to this book. Do yourself a favor—find everything that these two have ever written and read it.

We also wish to thank those who provided invaluable comments on this book at various stages of its life: Asher Sinensky, Kyle Erickson, Brendan Cooney (and the legal ninjas), Andy Oram, Nathan Good, and Seth Schoen.

Special thanks to the rest of the Privacy & Civil Liberties Engineering team at Palantir for acting as our research arm and teachers on all things privacy. Special thanks to the distinguished members of the Palantir Council of Advisors on Privacy and Civil Liberties (PCAP) for providing encouragement and fodder for this effort through so many enlightening discussions. Special thanks to the engineering teams at Palantir, for spending years imagining, building, and perfecting many of the architectures that we describe in this book. In a very real way, the authors are just the messengers, the documenters of the hard technical work that go into creating these systems.

Special thanks to Mike Loukides at O'Reilly for being as excited about this book as we were and helping us to make it happen. Inspiration for this book came out of meetings at O'Reilly's Foo Camp, specifically a session run by Brian Fitzpatrick and Harper Reed on Internet privacy in the post-Snowden era.

Courtney Bowman

To my co-authors, who enrich my working life with their erudition and passion for the content of this text, and whose company and good humor were the epidural to this protracted labor of love. To Kyle Erickson and especially Elissa Lerner for knowing when humor, gentle prodding, good-natured public shaming, and other more medieval editorial machinations were needed to prod me along; I quite literally would not have done it without your indefatigable encouragement. And, most of all, to Sarah, whose support, understanding, kindness, and unwavering affection remind me daily that the sacred spaces we aim to preserve and protect through privacy engineering matter most when the personhood cultivated therein can ultimately also be shared.

Ari Gesher

To my wife, for indulging yet another professional distraction that draws me out of our happy home and for taking care of the bedtimes that I'll miss while I'm out playing author. To my children: you are the inspiration for my wanting to make the world a better place to live in. Consider this a small part of my efforts to build a world that is safe for you to live in. To Chris Dibona and Tim O'Reilly for your encouragement, sometimes intentional and sometimes incidental. And to my parents: for never being impressed enough with my work to let me feel satisfied. You keep me moving. And finally, to my co-authors for tolerating my rewrites and doing the bulk of the work in writing this book.

John K. Grant

To Mike van Opstal, the engineer in my life. To my family and friends, who have to listen to me rant and rave on privacy and civil liberties on a daily basis and who hoped that this effort might purge my soul (no such luck). To Dr. Karp and Palantir for believing that privacy engineering could be a real job and letting me turn my passion into my life. To those who risk their lives every day to protect the ideals of a free society and labor to bring freedom to all those who want for it.

Daniel Slate

To my teachers, who shared with me the love of a good sentence. To my friends, Elissa Lerner and Kyle Erickson, from whom I have learned so much, and who, with their erudition, refined linguistic sensitivity, and dauntless persistence for excellence, made this a far better book than it would otherwise have been; they are as much authors of this book as any of us, regardless of what ended up on the cover page, and all should know this. To John, Ari, and Courtney, for their wisdom and good humor along the path of shared suffering. To my family and those who came before them who left the lands of tyranny to build lives of ordered creativity in a new, free land, and without whom none of this would have been possible.

Getting Started

You have decided to build a new technology that processes data about people. Where do you start? In Part I, we walk you through the initial steps that lay the foundation upon which your privacy-protective framework will be built. Chapter 1 defines the concept of privacy and the critical role of the engineer in shaping that concept through technology. We then raise some preliminary questions regarding when and how data is collected, which can be explored in great depth in privacy literature. While our book largely focuses on the management of data *after* it has been collected, data-collection considerations themselves do shape privacy architecture. We therefore provide a high-level discussion of data collection in Chapters 2 and 3. Finally, protecting data privacy necessarily involves ensuring that data is secure. Since the literature on information security techniques is substantial, Chapter 4 provides a basic discussion of the topic as background.

CHAPTER 1

What Is Privacy?

*Privacy incursions in the name of progress, innovation, and ordered liberty jeopardize the
continuing vitality of the political and intellectual culture that we say we value.*
—Julie E. Cohen, professor of law,
Georgetown University

Privacy is important. These three words comprise the philosophical compass for this
book, and summarize (albeit inelegantly) the eloquent description above regarding
the consequences of ignoring privacy. For us, privacy serves not only as a bulwark
against threats to individual liberty and society as we know it, but also as a cornerstone of a thriving economy rife with innovation.

There has long been and continues to be roiling societal debates on the topic of privacy. Every reader of this book will come with their own conception of why privacy is
important. What do you see as a threat to privacy? How significant are those threats?
And most importantly, what role will your technology play in shaping the world in
which those threats exist? If you are reading this book, then you have probably asked
yourself these questions and, in your own way, reached the same conclusion we have:
privacy is important.

Proceeding from that premise, we then assert that engineers can and should take privacy into account when designing and building technology. There is a long history of
interaction between policy and technology that demonstrates just how important a
role engineers can play. Thinking carefully about the architecture of privacy will show
that it is possible to build systems that make it substantially easier to protect privacy
and much more difficult to violate it, intentionally or otherwise. This book will help
you do that.

How to Think About Privacy

In order to build technology that can help protect privacy, we must first understand privacy and how it is shaped by law, policy, and technology. Though we often take its meaning for granted, privacy is neither a simple concept nor can it be assumed that everyone defines it the same way. Privacy can encompass a broad swath of sometimes interrelated and often overlapping ideas. It is also a moving target—the concept changes and adapts over time.

In this section, we define privacy for the purposes of this book. We also examine how technology has interacted with legal and policy development (and vice versa) to shape the concept of privacy. This is not meant to be a comprehensive history of privacy, but rather to provide some context to this complex interaction that will help you understand the broader environment in which your technology must operate.

Defining Privacy

A single definition of the word "privacy" has been historically difficult to pin down. Definitions of privacy have always been reflections of contemporary contexts, resulting, perhaps unsurprisingly, in what legal scholar Daniel Solove describes as a "concept in disarray."[1] Consequently, this concept can plausibly encompass no less than the "freedom of thought, control over one's body, solitude in one's home, control over personal information, freedom from surveillance, protection of one's reputation, and protection from searches and interrogations."[2]

Even documents regarded as essential bulwarks against encroachment on individual privacy turn out to be surprisingly vague on the topic. The United States Constitution, for instance, does not contain the actual word "privacy."[3] Other documents do not eschew the word, but they do not offer much help in defining it. The Universal Declaration of Human Rights, a component of the United Nations-created International Bill of Rights, asserts in Article 12 that "No one shall be subjected to arbitrary interference with his privacy." The European Convention on Human Rights, for its part, was only able to muster a "right to respect [the individual's] private and family life, his home and his correspondence." Consequently, it has been left to legislatures, courts, advocates, and academics to actually flesh out the elusive meaning behind these seven letters.

---

1 Solove, Daniel J. *Understanding Privacy*. Cambridge, Mass.: Harvard University Press, 2008.

2 Ibid.

3 In the United States, it was not until the 1960s, in *Griswold v. Connecticut*, that the U.S. Supreme Court identified a constitutional "right to privacy," opining that "specific guarantees in the Bill of Rights have penumbras, formed by emanations from those guarantees that help give them life and substance," and from those penumbras and emanations emerge "zones of privacy."

Broadly speaking, experts sort conceptions of privacy into two categories—*informational privacy*, which concerns "the collection, use, and disclosure of personal information," and *decisional privacy*, which relates to "the freedom to make decisions about one's body and family."[4] Given that this book focuses on technologies that work with data, we will concentrate our discussion on informational privacy. However, this should not be read to suggest that the adoption of these capabilities will only affect informational privacy. If information truly is power (as is frequently asserted), then the ability to control information about oneself can have a direct effect on the freedom one has to think and act independently. Thus, informational privacy cannot be wholly divorced from decisional privacy, and addressing one necessarily implicates the other.

A Short History of U.S. Informational Privacy

The concept of informational privacy has evolved over time. Tracing its history shows that the development of technology and privacy law and policy are closely intertwined. Changes in one area can have significant effects on the other. A historical review also illustrates how, in many cases, the same core issues we face today are merely the latest permutation of long-standing challenges. Understanding how informational privacy has developed in one jurisdiction will not only help us understand its current state but also its potential evolution in the future.[5]

More than 120 years before the seeming omnipresence of information-sharing platforms like Facebook, Instagram, Snapchat, and their kin, there was Kodak. In 1888, the Kodak camera was introduced to the American public, allowing anyone to capture and share moments of peoples' lives like never before. Concerns about the privacy implications of the new technology quickly followed. "Beware the Kodak," lamented *The Hartford Courant*, "The sedate citizen can't indulge in any hilariousness without incurring the risk of being caught in the act and having his photograph passed around among his Sunday School children."[6]

The legal community soon took notice. In 1890, Samuel Warren, a prominent Boston attorney, and Louis Brandeis, later to serve as a Supreme Court justice, published "The Right to Privacy" in the *Harvard Law Review* (*http://bit.ly/brandeis-right-privacy*), an article widely considered one of the most influential in the American

---

4 Solove, Daniel J., and Marc Rotenberg. *Information Privacy Law*. New York: Aspen Publishers, 2003 (emphasis ours).

5 Informational privacy law has also developed in Europe and around the world in different ways. A comprehensive history of the concept would, of course, have to consider a broader global lens. However, this section is not meant to be a comprehensive history of the concept—merely one case study of the interaction of the technical and policy/legal worlds.

6 Brayer, Elizabeth. *George Eastman: A Biography*. Baltimore: Johns Hopkins University Press, 1996. 71.

legal canon and still cited in court opinions to this day. The article began by briefly charting the development of the concept of privacy up until that point before determining "Recent inventions and business methods call attention to the next step which must be taken for the protection of the person…. Instantaneous photographs and newspaper enterprise have invaded the sacred precincts of private and domestic life…"[7] After outlining the perceived harms of these intrusions, Warren and Brandeis looked to the existing common law (i.e., law developed over time by judges as they decide cases) for the foundations of a "right to be let alone."[8] Notably, they also delineate limits to this right, suggesting that at some point "the dignity and convenience of the individual must yield to the demands of public welfare or of private justice."[9]

Thirty years later, Brandeis went on to erect yet another pillar in privacy history with what became one of the most frequently cited dissenting opinions in U.S. Supreme Court history (*http://bit.ly/brandeis-olmstead*). In 1928 in *Olmstead v. United States*, the Court determined in a 5–4 decision that federal agents could wiretap a phone without obtaining judicial approval. In a fiery dissent, Brandeis reaffirmed the importance of "the right to be let alone—the most comprehensive of rights and the right most valued by civilized men." Brandeis chided the majority that "time works changes, brings into existence new conditions and purposes" and therefore the Court must be prepared to apply constitutional protections to situations not envisioned by the Framers, which in this case meant applying the Fourth Amendment protections against unreasonable search and seizure beyond the "sanctities of a man's home." He warned that technology would continue to challenge the Court's conception of privacy protection. "The progress of science in furnishing the Government with means of espionage is not likely to stop with wiretapping," he wrote. "Ways may someday be developed by which the Government, without removing papers from secret drawers, can reproduce them in court, and by which it will be enabled to expose to a jury the most intimate occurrences of the home."

However, it would be nearly four decades before the Supreme Court would recognize Brandeis' prescience, and it would be an invention that had at that point already existed for more than 90 years, the telephone, which would inspire the Supreme Court to a new era of privacy protection. Noting that it could not "ignore the vital role that the public telephone has come to play in private communication," the Supreme Court, in *Katz v. United States* (1967), declined to follow the *Olmstead* majority's view that the Fourth Amendment be narrowly construed to apply only to the home, finding

---

7 Warren, Samuel D., and Louis D. Brandeis. "The Right to Privacy." *Harvard Law Review*, 1890.

8 Ibid.

9 Ibid.

instead that it "protects people, not places."[10] It therefore could protect activity conducted in areas accessible to the public from government surveillance (in this case, requiring a warrant for wiretapping a public telephone booth). The near-ubiquitous adoption of technology over the better part of a century had at last dragged the law forward.

By the 1960s, the growth of the post-New Deal government combined with the postwar economic and population boom resulted in an explosion in the number of records kept about people in both the government and private sector.[11] Computerized record-keeping, which had begun as early as the 1890 U.S. Census using Herman Hollerith's mechanical tabulator, was not just convenient—it was becoming essential as a means of managing an ever-increasing volume of data.

As data proliferated, academics and activists became increasingly concerned with how this data was being managed—particularly since much of it was then in the hands of the U.S. government and there was little transparency as to how it was being used. In 1972, the Secretary of the Department of Health, Education, and Welfare (HEW)[12] established the Secretary's Advisory Committee on Automated Personal Data Systems. It was formed to address "growing concern about the harmful consequences that may result from uncontrolled application of computer and telecommunications technology to the collection, storage, and use of data about individual citizens."[13] In assembling the Committee, Secretary Elliot Lee Richardson specifically cited technological innovation as the driver of this reassessment of privacy. "The use of automated data systems containing information about individuals is growing in both the public and private sectors...," he wrote. "The Department itself uses many such systems.... At the same time, there is a growing concern that automated personal data systems present a serious potential for harmful consequences, including infringement of basic liberties."

---

10 *Katz* established the "reasonable expectation of privacy" test to determine when the Fourth Amendment's protections apply. In applying the test, a court must consider whether a person subjectively believed that a location or situation is private, and then it must determine whether this belief would be generally recognized by society. This test remains a cornerstone of Fourth Amendment jurisprudence, and a full discussion of its strengths and weaknesses is beyond the scope of this book. Suffice it to say that its application became increasingly more complicated as the amount of information in the world—and the means of storing and sharing it—has multiplied at an astounding rate.

11 "The number of bank checks written, the number of college students, and the number of pieces of mail all nearly doubled; the number of income-tax returns quadrupled; and the number of Social Security payments increased by a factor of more than 35." HEW Report, Chapter 1, "Records and Record Keepers."

12 HEW later split into the Department of Health and Human Services and the Department of Education in 1979.

13 U.S. Dept. of Health, Education and Welfare, Secretary's Advisory Committee on Automated Personal Data Systems, Records, Computers, and the Rights of Citizens (*http://bit.ly/hew-1973-preface*), 1973. Preface.

In response, the Committee produced "Records, Computers and the Rights of Citizens," a (perhaps surprisingly) helpful government report that continues to influence privacy policy to this day. The report was submitted on June 25, 1973, the same day that John Dean, former White House Counsel, testified before the Senate Watergate Committee that President Richard Nixon was involved in the cover-up of the Watergate burglary. Allegations of governmental abuse of power pervaded the zeitgeist when the HEW Committee concluded that, "Under current law, a person's privacy is poorly protected against arbitrary or abusive record-keeping practices."

The Committee went on to propose a set of principles that should apply to the construction and use of automated personal data systems. These principles would eventually come to be known as the Fair Information Practice Principles (FIPPs), and they have been adopted around the world as the basic framework of information-privacy legislation and policy.

The FIPPs have been formulated in a variety of ways, and carry significant weight in the operational and technical frameworks of privacy. They are summarized in the following sidebar.

Fair Information Practice Principles (FIPPs)

Collection limitation
Do not collect more information than you need.

Data quality
You have a responsibility not to collect, store, and use inaccurate data.

Purpose specification
Tell people why you want their data and get their permission to use it that way.

Use limitation
Before you try to use already-collected data for an unexpected new purpose, explain why and get permission from the appropriate people.

Security
Protect the data you hold.

Openness
Be as transparent as possible to the people who entrust their data to you.

Individual participation
People should be able to see what you know about them and ask you to correct mistakes.

Accountability
You are liable for responsibly handling information.

These principles are now enshrined in such diverse places as the U.S. Privacy Act of 1974, the European Union Data Protection Directive, the Australian Privacy Act's Information Privacy Principles, the Singaporean Personal Data Protection Bill, India's Information Technology Rules (formally, The Reasonable Security Practices and Procedures and Sensitive Personal Data or Information Rules), and a number of other national laws and policies that make up today's privacy landscape.[14]

Today

The HEW report and the legislation that flowed from it over the course of two decades represent arguably the last major watershed moment in informational privacy law development. Since then, the legal infrastructure has been strained to the breaking point as policymakers and judges struggle to apply decades-old law to technology that was barely imaginable when those laws were passed.

The U.S. Privacy Act, for one, has not been substantially amended since its initial enactment in 1974, forcing innovators in data processing technology to figure out how to fit sophisticated new data structures into the filing cabinet-record paradigm that characterizes the Act. The Electronic Communications Privacy Act (ECPA), meanwhile, which governs U.S. federal law enforcement's use of wiretaps, pen registers, trap-and-trace devices, and the interception of electronic communications such as email, was enacted in 1986—long before most Americans had even heard of the Internet, let alone adopted it as one of their primary modes of communication and commerce. Consequently, ECPA has created a set of confusing, inconsistently applied standards, yielding strange results.[15]

U.S. state privacy laws have fared somewhat better, with states creating context-specific privacy requirements for an assortment of data types (e.g., bank records, insurance, educational information).[16] However, each state takes a different approach to privacy. When state laws conflict with federal laws, legislatures and courts are forced to engage in complex legal analysis to determine which system should take

---

14 It is important to note, however, that the FIPPs themselves are not legally binding, and the specifics of their incorporation into law and policy can vary from country to country and context to context. It's best to think of the FIPPs as representing general themes of privacy law, while still looking to specific law and policy to understand the actual legal requirements and limits for data collection and use in a particular location and industry.

15 For example, a single email is subject to multiple legal standards. Law enforcement has different procedures for getting access to an email depending on whether it is a) intercepted in transit, b) accessed from a server before it is 180 days old, or c) accessed after it has been on the server for 180 days. This is in contrast to a standard "snail mail" hard copy physical letter, where law enforcement has to get a warrant to read the letter no matter how old it is or where it happens to be in the process of transmission. Many people do not realize this about email—they assume it should have roughly the same protections as a regular letter as they are functionally equivalent. See ECPA Reform: Why Now? (*http://bit.ly/ddp-ecpa-reform*).

16 EPIC. "State Privacy Laws" (*http://bit.ly/epic-privacy-state*).

precedence. This often leads to confusing outcomes. Such a hodge-podge of privacy rules often leave multistate and multinational businesses scrambling for strategies to build one product or adopt one policy that meets the requirements of every state.

Meanwhile, the European Union's sometimes aggressive enforcement of assorted Member State "data protection" laws has led to stronger global privacy practices as multinational companies hoping to operate in Europe attempt to comply.[17] Yet even these laws are built on the foundation of the FIPPs, and are cracking under the strain of the new paradigm of contemporary data scale and complex analytics. The European Union has proposed an update to its data protection regime, which is discussed in more depth in Chapter 11.

Outside of legislatures, the courts have fared little better in trying to keep pace with technological development. In one of the more significant privacy decisions of the last twenty years, *Kyllo v. United States* (2001), the Supreme Court ruled that police would be required by the Fourth Amendment to obtain a search warrant in order to direct a thermal imaging device at a private residence. Acknowledging that "[i]t would be foolish to contend that the degree of privacy secured to citizens by the Fourth Amendment has been entirely unaffected by the advance of technology," the Court concluded that an unreasonable search has occurred because "here, the Government uses a device that is not in general public use, to explore details of the home that would previously have been unknowable without physical intrusion."

The Court's use of "not in general public use" could be read to suggest that the Court "deliberately adopted a rule that allows the outcome to change along with society," thereby trying to create a standard of privacy protection that adapts with the growth of technology.[18] But since there have been few follow-up cases along this line, it is hard to determine if the Court's rule was actually successful or if it just created more confusion without adding any real protection against intrusions on personal, informational privacy.

Lastly, the United States Federal Trade Commission (FTC) has taken on a lead role in protecting consumer privacy. It is worth noting that they have done so not under the auspices of any of the aforementioned privacy laws but rather pursuant to their authority under Section 5 of the Federal Trade Commission Act (*http://bit.ly/ftc-enforcing-privacy*) (15 USC 45), which prohibits "unfair or deceptive acts or practices in or affecting commerce." The FTC has used this authority to bring legal action

---

17 The term "data protection" is commonly used in Europe to describe policies and procedures that enable what we are referring to as "informational privacy" in this book. This is not meant to suggest a one-to-one correlation, as there are differences, and a deeper exploration of those nuances is beyond the scope of this book.

18 Kerr, Orin. "Can the Police Now Use Thermal Imaging Devices Without a Warrant? A Reexamination of Kyllo in Light of the Widespread Use of Infrared Temperature Sensors" (*http://bit.ly/volokh-kyllo*). The Volokh Conspiracy. January 4, 2010.

against organizations that they argue have deceived consumers by failing to live up to their promises to handle consumers' personal information in a secure way.

The FTC has developed such a reputation that some scholars have claimed that "today FTC privacy jurisprudence is the broadest and most influential regulating force on information privacy in the United States—more so than nearly any privacy statute or common law tort."[19] However, the overall effectiveness of these actions in providing more consumer privacy protection must be measured in light of the fact that it is primarily dependent on the FTC policing the organizations' assertions about their own behavior. This means the level of privacy protection is driven not by government regulation itself but by the organizations' decisions about the level of privacy protection they'd like to provide their own customers.

While law lurches along haphazardly, technology continues to leap forward. In 2013, the Pew Research Center's Internet & American Life Project reported that more than 90% of Americans owned cellular telephones, and some suggested that the adoption of the smartphone was outpacing the spread of any other technology in human history. The massive amount of transactional and geolocational data generated by these mobile devices contributes to the larger trend of an exponential growth in the amount of stored data in the world, which by one estimate reached around 1,200 exabytes in 2013.[20] Attempting to describe the state of the "big data" world in 2013, economists Viktor Mayer-Schönberger and Kenneth Cukier coined the term "*datafication*" to refer to "taking information about all things under the sun—including ones we never used to think of as information at all, such as a person's location, the vibrations of an engine, or the stress on a bridge—and transforming it into a data format to make it quantified [allowing] us to use the information in new ways." (See Chapter 11 for more on datafication.) An entire industry of big data analytics has emerged to take advantage of these mountains of information, often developing techniques that can extract unexpected insights (sometimes relating to deeply personal subjects) from seemingly innocuous data.

These vast reservoirs of data—in particular, personal data about individual behavior —have not only been a boon to the commercial sector, they have also provided a treasure trove of information for governments. Police departments, intelligence services, and government agencies of all kinds have harnessed the power of data analytics to do everything from eliminating inefficiencies in housing-code violation investigations to anticipating crime outbreaks to capturing terrorists. Privacy and civil liberties advocates have long expressed concern at the extent to which some of this informa-

---

19 Solove, Daniel J., and Woodrow Hartzog. "The FTC and the New Common Law of Privacy" (*http://bit.ly/solove-ftc*). *Columbia Law Review* 114, no. 3 (2014).

20 Mayer-Schönberger, Viktor, and Kenneth Cukier. *Big Data: A Revolution That Will Transform How We Live, Work, and Think*. London: John Murray, 2013. 9.

tion is being collected and used by governments, but for the most part they could only speculate as to what was happening behind the veil of secrecy shrouding the clandestine services.

This all changed on June 5, 2013, when *The Guardian* revealed the bulk collection of telephony data by the U.S. National Security Agency on a scale that shocked many observers.[21] Four days after breaking the news, *The Guardian* introduced the world to Edward Snowden, a former NSA contractor who executed one of the largest intelligence leaks in U.S. history in order to reveal "the federation of secret law, unequal pardon and irresistible executive powers that rule the world."[22] The ongoing release of classified materials has triggered one of the largest public discussions about privacy, and one of the most significant reviews of U.S. intelligence activity, since the Church Committee (*http://bit.ly/senate-church-comm*) investigated CIA and FBI domestic abuses in the 1970s.

Once more, the law is scrambling to catch up with new technological developments. A declassified opinion of the U.S. Foreign Intelligence Surveillance (FISA) Court, the body charged with judicial oversight of certain intelligence community activities, acknowledged as much when it found that Fourth Amendment protections did not apply to the collection of "non-content telephony metadata." It also suggested that this conclusion (which relied on a 1979 Supreme Court decision) would do well to be revisited by the Supreme Court "in the context of twenty-first century communications technology." Other courts have reached similar conclusions, and a robust debate over these issues continues in courtrooms, classrooms, and legislative hearing rooms around the world. While it remains unclear how these issues will be resolved in the coming years, it is clear that technological development will continue to be one of the driving forces in shaping an individual's privacy rights.

"East Coast" Code and "West Coast" Code

Technologists may think themselves helpless in the face of legal developments, resigned to waiting for society to react to a new technology and adapt law and policy to the new technological paradigm. In reality, technologists may have as much influence on the development of the law as the law does on technology. Consequently, the technology described in this book should not be thought of as just a *reaction* to the requirements of law but also as a potential means of *shaping* the ultimate legal outcomes.

---

21 Greenwald, Glenn. "NSA Collecting Phone Records of Millions of Verizon Customers Daily" (*http://bit.ly/nsa-verizon-data*). *The Guardian*. June 6, 2013.

22 Greenwald, Glenn, Ewen MacAskill, and Laura Poitras. "Edward Snowden: The Whistleblower behind the NSA Surveillance Revelations" (*http://bit.ly/guardian-snowden*). *The Guardian*. June 11, 2013.

As history illustrates, the interaction of privacy law and technological innovation can seem like billiard balls on a table. Often they appear to be largely separate worlds that occasionally collide, sending one or both careening off in a new direction, each one affecting the other in different ways but never merging. Inventors and engineers solder wires and write computer code, but their understanding of the law tends to be limited to the rules defining what they can and cannot do. Lawyers and policymakers, meanwhile, only become aware of new technology when it reaches a critical mass of usage in popular society, and they often spend years trying to understand how this new technology changes the world around them and then deciding how the law should (or should not) react to those changes.

However, we believe law and technology cannot and should not operate in separate worlds. Ideally they should work together, with technologists understanding and designing technology based on a solid grasp of relevant law and policy, and lawyers and policymakers understanding technological capabilities in order to better inform and even support their policy decisions. This concept derives from Harvard law professor Lawrence Lessig, who, in 1999, sought to explain the state of regulation in the nascent world of cyberspace:

> "The single most significant change in the politics of cyberspace is the coming of age of this simple idea: The code is law. The architectures of cyberspace are as important as the law in defining and defeating the liberties of the Net. Activists concerned with defending liberty, privacy or access must watch the code coming from the Valley —call it West Coast Code—as much as the code coming from Congress—call it East Coast Code."

Lessig later clarified further: "The lesson of *code is law* is not the lesson that we should be regulating code, the lesson of *code is law* is to find the right mix between these modalities of regulation to achieve whatever regulatory objective a government might be seeking."

The so-called "West Coast" code and "East Coast" code can interact in a variety of ways.[23] In some cases, "West Coast" code defines the physics of the world in which "East Coast" code can operate. The very design of devices and the networks that support them establishes the boundaries of the environment within which policymakers can operate. For example, the creation of biometric authentication technology allows policymakers to require the use of such capabilities to secure sensitive systems. In other cases, "East Coast" code directly limits what "West Coast" code can do. For example, cybercrime laws prohibit the creation of malicious code. It is the complex spectrum between these two extremes that generates the sizeable range of options available to the thoughtful, privacy-minded software engineer.

---

23 Although Lessig sets his metaphor in terms of U.S. geography, his underlying point about the interaction between those who make policy and those who write code is universal.

Consider the development of cellular phone capabilities. Back in ancient times, cell phones were relatively simple devices used to connect two people for a voice conversation. Today, they can contain (and generate) substantial amounts of information touching almost every aspect of our lives. Cell phones can now store gigabytes of information in the form of documents, pictures, videos, and other types of files. They can also run various applications that allow them to access other troves of information such as server-based email accounts.

While useful and driven by consumer desire for such access, the storage of this data has led to some challenging new issues under U.S. Fourth Amendment "search and seizure" law, and the development of certain cell phone capabilities can have a profound effect on personal privacy and fundamental freedoms. The Fourth Amendment to the U.S. Constitution prohibits agents of the government from conducting "unreasonable searches and seizures" of "persons, houses, papers, and effects" without a judicially issued warrant based on a finding that there is "probable cause" to believe that evidence of a crime or contraband will be found. There are several judicially created exceptions to this stricture, including one that has been interpreted to allow law enforcement officers to seize cell phones as part of a search incident to arrest and review the contents of those phones without obtaining a search warrant.

For a long time, courts were split over the validity of these searches. Some have suggested that because the phone is on the arrestee's person and may contain evidence, seizing the phone constitutes little more than reading the contents of a piece of paper found in the arrestee's pockets. Others have argued that the sheer volume of information available on the device changes the analysis, as law enforcement officers would normally only be able to obtain such extensive information via warrants that authorize the search of a computer hard drive or subpoenas requesting access to stored emails from a third-party email provider. Eventually in 2014, the Supreme Court, in *United States v. Riley* settled this question, finding a substantial distinction between the contents of one's pockets and the contents of one's cell phone:

> "Modern cell phones, as a category, implicate privacy concerns far beyond those implicated by the search of a cigarette pack, a wallet, or a purse. A conclusion that inspecting the contents of an arrestee's pockets works no substantial additional intrusion on privacy beyond the arrest itself may make sense as applied to physical items, but any extension of that reasoning to digital data has to rest on its own bottom."

Thus, we can see that "West Coast" decisions to create devices with substantial storage capacity has required "East Coast" counterparts to reconsider long-standing legal doctrines.

Another thorny issue surrounds geolocational data generated by cellular phones. Geolocational information can be generated any time a phone call is made, any time a text is sent, any time an application relies on geolocation data (e.g., an application providing information on vehicle traffic), and even any time a device passively "pings" a cellular tower as it moves in and out of coverage areas. This information can be stored on the phone, with the cellular provider, and with the maker of the application, thus creating a potentially enormously valuable data source for law enforcement and intelligence agencies.

But this body of information exists *because* of "West Coast" decisions to design systems that generate and store it. "East Coast" law enforcement and intelligence policymakers then responded to the creation of this entirely new set of data by integrating it into their investigatory techniques. Ultimately, the public, courts, and policymakers are left to debate and decide if this is an appropriate use of the data, and whether there should be legal restrictions on the use of this information both by the public and private sectors. In this case, the "West Coast" code created an entirely new source of information that fundamentally changed the relationship of the individual users to their devices (we now essentially carry tracking devices in our pockets) and it was done in a relative "East Coast" code vacuum, thereby creating a great deal of uncertainty regarding the power of the government and others to track our every move.

These are just two examples that serve to illustrate the complexity of the technological and legal landscape, and in many ways, even these cases are overly simplified. "West Coast" and "East Coast" are hardly monoliths defined by a single motivation or goal. Instead, they are both composed of constantly shifting coalitions of interests, including individual coders motivated sometimes by profit and sometimes by altruism; businesses with substantial economic stakes in both legal and technical outcomes; policymakers torn between protecting privacy, preventing crime and threats to national security, and promoting economic growth in the tech sector; advocacy organizations looking to foster a free and independent cyber world while at the same time trying to curb the potential for nefarious exploitation of this world; and individual consumers eager to take advantage of useful and fun new technologies while anxiously trying to preserve a seemingly dwindling sphere of private life. Each of these interests can and often do shift from looking to either "West Coast" code or "East Coast" code to address any given concern.

Why Privacy Is Important

The historical influence of technology on privacy law raises the question—did technological innovators have privacy in mind when they designed their products? When George Eastman introduced the Kodak camera, how much thought did he give to its ultimate effect on individual privacy? Did he imagine a world of candid, snapshot photography and wonder how it would affect, for better or for worse, the photographer and the photographed? Did he hesitate for a moment before pulling away the cloth to unveil his invention? Did he consider ways to modify the technology to better protect privacy?

Perhaps the better question to consider is why Eastman, or any technological innovator, would even want to consider these questions in the first place. In today's society, at least, there are a number of potentially significant consequences—both practical and ethical—for businesses that fail to consider the privacy implications of their work.

On the practical side, innovators today face a complex web of privacy law at the state, federal, and international levels. Failure to comply with these laws can open the door to sizeable civil lawsuits, or substantial government fines. Here are just a few recent examples:

- In 2011, Facebook settled a class action lawsuit for $20 million for using the names and pictures of members in "Sponsored Stories" without their consent. Facebook has also agreed to aggressive oversight from the U.S. FTC that could lead to further fines if the company is found to share user information without proper notice and consent.

- Google settled with the FTC in 2012 for $22.5 million for bypassing the privacy settings of the Safari mobile browser. In addition, Google has been fined by a number of European data-protection authorities (and is under investigation by several others) for violation of privacy laws.

- Smaller businesses are not immune. In 2013, the makers of a social networking application called Path were fined $800,000 by the FTC for collecting personal information from children without parental consent.

- A four-employee smartphone application developer called W3 Innovations agreed to a $50,000 fine paid to the FTC for similar violations involving the collection and sharing of data from children.

Steep fines like these create incentives to build or buy products that can facilitate the privacy-protective practices demanded by regulators. But aside from financial penalties, companies might also be in the market for such products to help proactively assuage the concerns of a privacy-sensitive customer base. Any customer with sensitive data will likely prefer a product or a service provider that can keep their information safe from theft or misuse, and otherwise handle data appropriately. Innovators could also favor privacy-protective products to circumvent any bad publicity that might doom a new product before it ever has a chance to flourish.

Government organizations and the businesses selling to them, will face similar pressures. Statutes, regulations, and policy can all require the implementation of complex data-handling procedures. Meanwhile, public opinion can sometimes demand the implementation of privacy-protective measures before data-driven programs can win broad support. The product designers who anticipate these considerations as they build their offerings will often have a business advantage over those who have not incorporated privacy-protective technologies into their core design.

Another practical consideration is the need to hire the best talent. Most companies will only be as good as their engineering talent, and many of those engineers will want to be challenged by their work. Engineers want to work at companies at the vanguard of their respective fields, and innovative data privacy solutions are part of what is considered the cutting edge—this alone may prove attractive.

But there is the ethical component to consider as well. Engineers working for a company that is regularly implicated in privacy violations or that sells its product to companies or countries that might misuse that technology may not only potentially face the pricking of their own conscience but also the disapproval of their fellow engineers. This latter point should not be taken lightly. In robust online communities in which many play an active part, reputation is paramount. A company that dedicates itself to doing business in a way that enhances privacy protection at best, and at the very least does no harm to individual privacy, may have an easier time appealing to engineering talent.

Finally, technologists may wish to take steps to protect their users' privacy if for no reasons other than (1) to acknowledge and respect the trust their customers place in them, and (2) to recognize that they, too, must live in the same world that their products will shape, and will face the same harm as their fellow citizens would from inadequate privacy protections. Engineers should not divest themselves of responsibility for the societal consequences of the technology they create.

While there may be no absolute "right" answer in terms of how much privacy each of us should have and how that privacy should be preserved, we argue that it is unacceptable for engineers to take an agnostic view—either by choosing to ignore the effects of their technological designs or by simply remaining ill-informed as to the potential political, economic, and social effects of their products. Given their power as agents of change (a subject whose surface is merely scratched by this chapter), engineers have a responsibility to the rest of society.

In a liberal democratic society, social accountability with regard to privacy must be a part of technological development. Technologists must do their best to protect privacy—by maintaining familiarity with important policy decisions and ongoing court cases, learning to use the latest tools available, or building new ones themselves. These concerns are not just academic. Ignoring them can have devastating costs to business and society, and implementing them can yield enormous practical rewards.

Before You Get Started

Since Warren and Brandeis' first, relatively short law review article appeared in the *Harvard Law Review* over a century ago, countless volumes have been written on the right to privacy. Dozens of privacy conferences convene around the world every year, each devoted to trying to understand this elusive right and how to best preserve it (see "Selected Privacy Conferences" in Chapter 12). This chapter can therefore hardly do justice to this ever-growing trove of privacy scholarship, but we hope it at least provides a high-level understanding of how technology and privacy interact and the important role technologists play in that nexus.

With some background on these issues now in mind, you can start thinking about how you might determine which privacy capabilities to use, and when. A series of basic questions about the technology you are trying to build will help get you started:

Does this technology interact with personally identified or identifiable information?
Define your data sets. If they contain personally identified or identifiable (PII) data, then you need to dig deeper into whether or not privacy-protective features should be incorporated into the design. As we'll see in Chapter 2, PII is readily defined, but determining whether information is identifiable requires deeper analysis. Remember, users of a system are not operating in a vacuum—they exist in a world of data. Just because the data used by your product is not identifiable in itself does not mean users cannot still match that data with other data from outside the system, thereby rendering the data identifiable.[24]

What is the technology supposed to do with the data?
As the product designer, you will of course already have this in mind. But since you are defining the parameters of your privacy analysis, it's important to remember that you are building something that has a primary goal beyond—and most likely totally unrelated to—privacy. Just about anything that uses PII involves some conscious decision by users to provide personal information (read: give up some privacy) in order to receive some utility from the product.[25] Consequently, your concern about privacy should not be so absolute as to undermine this transaction by not providing the full utility expected by your end user. When starting design, it will prudent to think through the tradeoffs between privacy and other benefits, weighing where you should you set the dividing line and what should be the defaults.

---

24 Preventing re-identification can be quite challenging, with some analysts and scholars suggesting re-identification will be more likely and normal than our current intuitions suggest. See, for example, Ohm, Paul. "Broken Promises of Privacy: Responding to the Surprising Failure of Anonymization" (*http://bit.ly/ssrn-ohm-privacy*). *UCLA Law Review*, 57 (2010): 1701.

25 Obviously the transaction is not always so simple. On the one hand, law enforcement and intelligence systems, for example, do not always involve a known sharing of data about oneself, but—at least in a democratic society—popular control of the government means that at a societal level a decision was made to give these organizations the power to collect and utilize this information for the larger benefit of safety and order. On the other hand, users' decisions to share data are not always so deliberate, as demonstrated by the large numbers of users who express shock upon learning that their online activities were even recorded, let alone stored, processed, and analyzed. Moreover, claims to consent and oversight can seem dubious when considering databases and data-collection activities whose very existence is secret. This can also occur in the private sector, as with Flash cookies, user-agent profiling, recording WiFi probe packets, and so on.

What could the technology do with the data?

Once your product ships or is downloaded or otherwise gets into the hands of your customers, you lose some degree of control over it. They are going to use it for what it was designed to do, but they are not necessarily going to be constrained by the parameters of the product documentation. You have to consider these potential other uses and make sure you control for them as much as possible. Could the data that is collected or used by the capability be used to reveal sensitive information that users had no intention of exposing? Could different types of data be uploaded into the application and used in a privacy-threatening way? Never underestimate the creativity (and the tenacity) of talented technical people—if there's an unconventional way to use your product, someone will find it. Try to think two moves ahead of them.

What are the potential privacy concerns?

Create a three-column chart. In the first column, list the potential functions of your product (both intended and unintended). In the second column, list all the potential privacy concerns raised by each function. In some cases, these concerns will track to particular laws or policies (e.g., European Union data protection laws). In other cases, the concerns will reflect other interests, such as your own organizational values, or the knowledge that consumers will respond negatively to certain consequences. Never discount your own instincts as to whether an outcome feels "creepy," even if you can find no legal or other imperative that prohibits a particular usage of the product.

How can you configure your privacy building blocks to address those issues?

In the third column, find a privacy mitigation strategy for each privacy concern. As you think through this part of the framework, do *not* start with the technical solution; it's almost impossible to design privacy protections that function entirely independently of human control. Instead, technical capabilities must *support human-managed policy* that is designed to protect privacy. Imagine the individual user or corporate or government privacy officer trying to use your product. How would they want to protect their privacy interests? What tools would they need in order to effectively manage their data and address privacy concerns? Are they more likely to want to establish rigid preventive measures to ensure data is never used in certain ways or are they more likely to use oversight mechanisms that discourage data misuse by ensuring accountability? Then fill in the third column with the technical building blocks that will enable this policy outcome.

Answering these questions should provide a basic framework for how your technology might interact with the rest of the world. These questions will also help you figure out who needs to see what data and when they need to see it as information is processed. This information will help you begin to sketch out the basic architectural framework upon which you can hang your privacy-enhancing features.

But don't start building just yet. Next, start considering questions regarding the potential privacy implications of your technology:

- Is it creating or storing new types of data that might expose new facets of an individual's life?
- Would exposure of this information cause embarrassment, lead to stigmatization of or discrimination against the individual, or even just inconvenience or annoyance?
- Does the creation and/or use of this data change the balance of power between individuals, businesses, or governments?
- Does this data fundamentally change how these interests interact in a way that creates advantages and/or disadvantages for any of them?

In addition to these basic questions, don't dismiss your gut instinct as to whether the use of a new capability might be perceived as "creepy"—a standard that is largely undefinable yet often instantly recognizable.

If the answer to these questions is "yes" (or if you have that creepy feeling in your gut), then you need to make two fundamental decisions:

- Should I build this? Do I believe the benefits of this technology outweigh the potential privacy risks it creates?
- How do I build this in a way that mitigates those risks?

The first question is one you will need to determine yourself. The second is one we hope you can answer with the help of this book.

CHAPTER 2

Personal Data and Privacy

Any architectural considerations regarding data-privacy protections begin the moment the data is collected. Privacy issues must be addressed at all stages of the data life cycle—from collection to storage to analysis to action (not to mention the periods when data is no longer being used: archival, purging, and destruction). We will start at the beginning.

Good practices in both information security and data collection are *necessary*, though not *sufficient*, to implement privacy protections. Parts II and III of this book will describe a set of useful practices and controls for implementing privacy protections. However, designing privacy protections is about limiting harm by authorized users— those that have been explicitly granted access to the data for some purpose. But what about *unauthorized* access to data? All of the privacy controls in the world are meaningless if they can be circumvented from the start. Information security, therefore, is about limiting unauthorized access to data, and is fundamental to building a privacy-protective system.

Meanwhile, all of the privacy controls in the world (and any information security built to protect them) are useless if administered to irresponsibly collected data. Protecting privacy means data must be handled responsibly at every step of the process that moves it from the initial point of collection to its ultimate home in a privacy-protected data store.

On the topic of data collection, consider this a brief overview of useful questions and best practices; on the topic of information security, this is just the tip of the iceberg.

Data Collection: Understanding Privacy's First Frontier

Separate from questions surrounding system security are questions regarding responsible data collection, or, plainly: the generation or recording of data about people—both individual and aggregate.

"Data about people" is a pretty broad description. And in practice, this can take many forms. Some common examples:

- Emails on a service provider's servers
- Voicemails on a service provider's servers
- Web-server logs
- User-submitted information from a web form
- Crash reports submitted to a central server
- Digitized paper forms
- Uploaded photos
- Phone call metadata
- Sniffed network traffic
- Financial transaction data
- Recorded medical imaging data
- Closed-circuit television recordings
- Location-tracking database on a smartphone
- Location-tracking database on a cell tower

Characterization and provenance of data will be significant factors in determining handling procedures. We can start thinking about the problem by broadly separating considerations into two very different considerations:

Policy
> The *what* and *why* of data collection.

Implementation
> The *how* of the collection process itself. This part is about making sure the technical reality implements policy decisions correctly.

Policy Considerations

The easiest way to avoid protecting sensitive data is to abstain from collecting it in the first place. In privacy circles, this is known as *proportionality*—the practice of only collecting and retaining what's necessary to accomplish a stated goal. Proportionality exists in tension with the current practice of many companies that are interested in collecting as much data as possible and are working under the assumption that all data is valuable, even if its value is not apparent at the time of collection.

Proportionality starts with identifying the use cases for the proposed collected data. Once the use cases have been clearly described, the actual data needed to support them can be pinpointed. With the necessary data defined, collection mechanisms can be built to filter out data that is not tied to a clear use case, and non-relevant information can be quickly removed during analysis. In addition, for use cases that need to generate aggregates of individual records and have no need for the source data, calculating the aggregate on the fly is a good way to minimize the amount of sensitive data that is held. For example, if you were building a system to calculate the average length of a phone call on a phone system, the call record itself (including phone numbers, locations, devices used, etc.) can be immediately discarded once its duration is added to the calculation of the global average.

At the limit, it's possible to design your overall system in such a way that certain parts of the data in the system are made inherently uncollectable by a central authority using cryptography. The recent changes to Apple's iMessage system, which now encrypts the message data in a manner that Apple cannot decrypt, is a good example of this. This sort of cryptography can preempt concerns about being compelled to by an external authority to collect more data than was originally intended by making compelled collection impossible.

Homomorphic Encryption

One promising new technique that could radically transform the policy and practice of privacy engineering is *homomorphic encryption*. Homomorphic encryption systems can do calculations on encrypted data without needing to first decrypt the data. The results of the calculations are delivered encrypted to the client, completely opaque to the system performing the calculations. This is achieved by using a cryptographic system whose encrypted form (cipherext) obeys certain mathematical relationships. For example, multiplication of the ciphertext produces a new ciphertext that is equivalent to decrypting the ciphertext, applying the same multiplication to the plaintext, and then re-encrypting the resulting plaintext.

Various crypto systems are gaining in popularity and are becoming increasingly sophisticated. RSA, a popular crypto system, is already homomorphic over multiplication. Moreover, in 2009, researchers at Stanford and IBM were able to create a system that is homomorphic over both multiplication and addition. This is notable because multiplication and addition can be composed to implement any Boolean logic circuit, enabling a large universe of calculations to be performed. Given such a system, it's theoretically possible to do any arbitrary transformation or search of encrypted data without revealing anything about the underlying plaintext data.

Operationally, this means all the data in a system could reside, encrypted, on a third-party system (like a virtual private server (VPS) in a cloud host provider's infrastructure). This system could be used to perform various calculations on the encrypted data without ever having the data exist in unencrypted plaintext on the system. Not only does this protect the data on the host at all times from interception and eavesdropping, but it also means one could operate a service that never needs access to plaintext. Taken to its logical extreme, this means it's theoretically possible to operate a service that operates on data that never has any access to its unencrypted form. This would essentially drop the need for traditional data collection to zero. One could imagine medical diagnosis-as-a-service or tax-preparation-as-a-service where the service provider only operates on homomorphically encrypted data and never has any access to the sensitive personal details involved in these pursuits.

A good example of a simple analysis on the privacy-enhancing possibilities would be Google's Gmail system, a free webmail service that shows its users ads based on the contents of their emails. While Google maintains that humans never see the private content of your emails, the fact that the content is digested by a machine makes some people feel their privacy has been violated. Using homomorphic encryption, the users' email could be submitted to the ad-selection algorithm in encrypted form. The algorithm would then run over the encrypted data and produce the ad to be placed at the top of the user's screen. While it's possible to infer something about the user's email given the choice of ad, a system like this preserves more privacy, as the contents of the emails are never seen by the algorithms themselves.

Unfortunately, in practice, it seems that homomorphic encryption is a long way off. At the time of this writing (2015), current implementations require something on the order of billion-to-a-trillion more computations than their non-encrypted analogs. There are a few vendors working on bringing more efficient systems to market, but for the foreseeable future, homomorphic encryption will only be useful for performing highly sensitive but computationally cheap calculations.

Once you've decided to collect data, a myriad of laws covering wiretapping, telecommunications, employment, health care, and others may apply to any particular set of data, depending on the context of the collection. Even more basic factors, such as the physical location of the collection and the storage of the data, can shape the ultimate legal mosaic that will govern your data system. Don't be fooled by so-called "open source" data—just because data is available through a Google search does not mean there are no rules associated with collecting and analyzing it. The scope of the initial collection may create significant risk and liability for you, and may impose a number of architectural limitations on the ultimate design of your system. It's important to talk to a legal expert to make sure you understand the rules that will apply to the data in your organization, and to do so before you build your system.

The United States and the European Union both have a legal concept of personal data, which is a piece of information that can be used to identify or distinguish an individual.

In the U.S., this is known as personally identifiable information (PII). Defined by the National Institute of Standards and Technology, PII is "any information about an individual maintained by an agency, including (1) any information that can be used to distinguish or trace an individual's identity, such as name, social security number, date and place of birth, mother's maiden name, or biometric records; and (2) any other information that is linked or linkable to an individual, such as medical, educational, financial, and employment information."[1]

In the E.U., personal data is defined as "any information relating to an identified or identifiable natural person (*data subject*); an identifiable person is one who can be identified, directly or indirectly, in particular by reference to an identification number or to one or more factors specific to his physical, physiological, mental, economic, cultural or social identity."[2]

PII is *any information that correlates directly to an individual.* A name, social security number, driver's license number, national ID number, phone number, and email address are all examples of commonly recognized PII. However, there is no universal agreement on what constitutes PII. For example, under U.S. law, an IP address is not considered PII, but under E.U. law, it is.

Furthermore, other data points, though not necessarily tied to an individual, nevertheless may be considered a strong enough indicator of identity to merit heightened protection. Some examples include:

- SIM card integrated circuit card identifier (ICCID) numbers
- SIM card international mobile subscriber identity (IMSI) numbers
- Mobile equipment identifier (MEID) numbers
- Advertising network cross-site cookies
- Automobile license plate numbers
- WiFi media access control (MAC) addresses
- Bluetooth MAC addresses

---

1 McCallister, Erika, Tim Grance, and Karen Scarfone. *Guide to Protecting the Confidentiality of Personally Identifiable Information (PII) Recommendations of the National Institute of Standards and Technology* (*http://bit.ly/nist-pii*). Gaithersburg, MD: U.S. Dept. of Commerce, National Institute of Standards and Technology, 2010.

2 "Directive 95/46/EC of the European Parliament and of the Council of 24 October 1995 on the protection of individuals with regard to the processing of personal data and on the free movement of such data" (*http://bit.ly/eu-pii*).

Previously, data collectors could purge all personal identifiers from a data set relatively easily and consider a data set free of any privacy concerns. However, in the age of big data, anonymization may not be enough. The distinction between PII and non-PII has begun to blur. It's now possible to take data devoid of any personal identifiers and identify individuals by joining it with other data sets until a clear picture of identity emerges, a process known as *re-identification*.

Imagine, for example, information about patients in a clinical trial for a new medication. By removing the names, addresses, and other personal identifiers from the dataset, the data owners could make the data available to medical researchers and assume zero privacy risk. However, the clinical trial data may have information about other medications the participants are taking. By combining the clinical trial patient data with pharmacy records or medical histories, it's possible to reidentify the otherwise anonymized patient data.[3]

The data-collection implications are therefore twofold. First, if you're collecting data that meets the classic definition of PII, make sure to implement privacy controls throughout the data-collection process. Second, a good operational definition of what constitutes PII is rather expansive, and you should consider if your collected data is only one joined data set away from revealing personal information.

In the past few decades, changes in technology have far outpaced the legislatures, and courts, response to it. As a result, there are new types of data collection that do not violate the letter of the law but may violate the spirit of privacy protections enshrined in existing laws. Responsible technologists should therefore be especially aware of privacy considerations when collecting and using data in legal gray areas.

One such gray area concerns the public and private sector uses of automated license plate reader data (ALPR). ALPR technology entails the use of cameras to capture license-plate images (along with time, date, and geolocation information) associated with vehicles on public streets. These cameras can be mounted at stationary locations or on moving vehicles. They are currently operated by several state and local law enforcement agencies as well as private sector companies (which in turn often sell this data to government agencies). Depending on the number of cameras in place and the sophistication of the analytics applied to this data, ALPR systems can reveal detailed information about the movement of individuals and draw potentially sensitive conclusions from that information, such as whether or not the driver of the vehicle attends a church, frequents a gay bar, or participates in a political protest. However, because a license plate is plainly visible to anyone standing on a public

---

3 As legal scholar and technologist Paul Ohm noted in "Broken Promises of Privacy: Responding to the Surprising Failure of Anonymization" (*http://bit.ly/uclalaw-ohm-broken*), privacy regulations and practices based on the notion of anonymization may now be untenable given the realities of modern data processing.

street, the law does not yet distinguish between ordinary viewing and automated viewing. Collection and use of ALPR data remains permissible for now.

Drivers are likely not fully aware of the scope of potential information that could be collected, gleaned, and inferred about them as they traverse public streets. These reasonable expectations of individual privacy should be kept in mind by technology developers and early adopters when building these systems, and reasonable steps to protect and anticipate privacy should be taken as the law considers and adjusts to technological innovation.

Implementation Considerations

Even with a carefully considered data-collection policy that addresses the questions above, oversights in architecture can create a system that behaves, albeit unintentionally, contrary to your policy. Here are some issues to consider when designing the technical implementation of a system—two important ones to avoid, and an important one to include.

At the point of collection, it's often easiest to make entire copies of the data's present form. For example, if you were building a system to analyze a social network as defined by email connections inside a corporate network, your point of collection would likely be one of the mail servers through which all the mail in the network flows. Although your analysis of who contacts whom would only require header information (which is metadata) and not the actual body of emails, it might be easier to store copies of the messages themselves, including the message bodies (which is content). But even if you restrict yourself to just email headers, some headers may include the originating IP address in addition to the subject line, both of which could be considered sensitive.

Whenever it's impossible or extremely impractical to avoid collecting the non-essential data at all, opt for minimization procedures that strip the data down for just the task at hand and ideally, nothing more. For the email example, the only data that would need to be recorded would be the sender and receiver information, and possibly a timestamp (for time-weighted decay of the social network links).

The initial point of data collection is often not the same as the place of its ultimate storage. In some cases, the data passes through several steps on its journey, including transmission, copying, and transformation, before ending up in its system-of-record. Along the way, one or more intermediate copies of the data may be made, and these copies must also be kept safe.

The most direct approach would be to encrypt the data at the point of collection and make sure it remains that way until (or even after) it is housed in its final system with appropriate privacy controls. If the data is encrypted from the point of collection, you don't need to rely on the access controls and security of the systems housing intermediate copies in transmission.

But if initial encryption isn't possible, intermediate copies should be subject to, at minimum, the same rigorous protections as the final system. This protection must apply to copies of the data that are stored in durable storage (like a disk), and in memory on shared-access multiuser systems, and as data are transmitted over plaintext, unencrypted network links.

Make sure to audit your architecture to trace every location that stores a copy of the data in transit, and consider whether or not the security regime is more or less permissive than the system-of-record. An insecure system may allow the circumvention of correctly applied access controls such as filesystem permissions. Copies might be made outside of your data collection flow such as a system-level backup process. When you purge these copies, make sure to use secure deletion practices such as writing over the original data with random bytes. (This is also a good opportunity to engage with your InfoSec resources.)

Once data lands in a larger repository, it may become difficult to identify or establish the source and context of the original acquisition of that data. Tagging (i.e., appending additional metadata that provides more information about the raw data) can often offset that risk.

As you collect data, tagging it with basic details about when and where it was collected will simplify the task of those ultimately managing the data. Metadata allows users to quickly sort data for access control and other purposes. The more metadata you can add to provide future users with useful context (e.g., a record of consent by the data subject for certain uses), the more options you give those users for managing that data.

Conclusion

Data collection is where the chain of custody for data begins. A careful analysis of the policy considerations, with regard to both legal regulations and the inherent intention of the system owners, is necessary to understand the sensitivity and privacy risk embodied in collecting data. From that understanding, you can begin to assess which data to collect (and which not to collect) and how to handle it responsibly once it's collected. Finally, care must be taken at the outset with your technical implementation in order to avoid common pitfalls in the collection pipeline that can compromise privacy protections, and to preserve the metadata collection that will enable fine-grained privacy controls later in the data's life cycle.

CHAPTER 3

Case Studies in Data Collection

Data collection is hard—even experienced engineering teams sometimes fail to build systems that express their intentions correctly. Here are a few real-world examples of high-profile systems that didn't adequately account for the privacy considerations inherent in data collection.

Google Street View WiFi: Inadvertent Over-Collection of Data

Google's Street View uses information gathered by specially outfitted cars to produce extremely detailed maps of city streets around the world. Along with street photography tied to GPS tracked data, the Google Street View cars were also recording WiFi signals. The growing database of the location of the world's wireless networks aided mobile phones in determining their position faster than a GPS satellite fix alone could provide.

However, the Street View cars were not just mapping out the location of the WiFi networks but actually recording and storing snippets of network traffic. Any time the WiFi antennas on the Street View cars picked up unsecured WiFi traffic, individual 802.11x Ethernet frames were captured. These recorded frames included not just the headers that specified the name or SSID of the network (which was all the information Google needed to map the network), but also the full contents of that frame, meaning any and all data being transmitted. Depending on how the users accessed the Internet, this may have included things like passwords and full email messages.

Google became aware of this problem in 2010 after a data-protection authority in Germany asked to audit the data they were collecting on WiFi networks.

"As soon as we became aware of this problem, we grounded our Street View cars and segregated the data on our network, which we then disconnected to make it inaccessible," Google wrote on its blog. "We want to delete this data as soon as possible, and are currently reaching out to regulators in the relevant countries about how to quickly dispose of it. Maintaining people's trust is crucial to everything we do, and in this case we fell short."

Google then outlined the steps it would be taking in asking a third party to review the relevant software, confirming deletion of the data, and reviewing internal procedures to address similar problems in the future. They also ended the practice of collecting WiFi network data via Street View cars.[1]

Google acknowledged that it was a mistake carried over by experimental code written in 2006, and stated it had no intention to collect or use such payload data. Presumably, if Google was aware of exactly what was being collected by the Street View cars, they would have not collected the full frames at all, or immediately performed a minimization process to purge all the captured except for the MAC address, SSID name, and its corresponding GPS location.

As of mid-2015, there is still pending litigation against Google for this mistake. Google's error underscores the importance of aggressive oversight of data-collection processes to ensure data intake is consistent with the goals of the program and with privacy law and policy. It's never safe to assume a collection system is going to perform flawlessly.

iPhone Location Database

When Apple released iOS 4 in June 2010, it included a new, silent feature on all iPhones running the newest version of their mobile operating system. The list of every location visited by each iPhone was now recorded in a file named `consolidated.db`. Discovered by Alasdair Allen and Pete Warden, this finding was presented at the *Where 2.0* conference in April 2011. From their original blog post on the subject:

> "This contains latitude-longitude coordinates along with a timestamp. The coordinates aren't always exact, but they are pretty detailed. There can be tens of thousands of data points in this file, and it appears the collection started with iOS 4, so there's typically around a year's worth of information at this point. Our best guess is that the location is determined by cell-tower triangulation, and the timing of the recording is erratic, with

---

1 "WiFi Data Collection: An Update" (*http://bit.ly/google-wifi-data*). Official Google Blog. May 14, 2010.

a widely varying frequency of updates that may be triggered by traveling between cells or activity on the phone itself."[2]

According to Apple, this was not exactly a record of the locations the phone had been. Instead, it was actually a copy of crowd-sourced location information to aid the phone in rapidly geolocating itself faster than it could using just a GPS satellite signal (which sometimes takes minutes to compute). Using anonymous data submissions from everyone's iPhones, Apple had created a large database recording the location of cell towers and WiFi networks. Each individual phone would download a subset of the cache to speed up the time it would take to get a location fix in a matter of seconds.[3]

The completeness of the database—which appeared to be holding about 10 months of location data—was due to (according to Apple) a software bug that would never remove data downloaded into the cache. When operating correctly, the phone was only supposed to hold seven days of location database cache rather than a seemingly permanent record of every location the phone had visited.

Apple fixed the perceived problems with this feature in a subsequent iOS update:

> "**Software Update** Sometime in the next few weeks Apple will release a free iOS software update that:
>
> - reduces the size of the crowd-sourced Wi-Fi hotspot and cell tower database cached on the iPhone,
> - ceases backing up this cache, and
> - deletes this cache entirely when Location Services is turned off.
>
> In the next major iOS software release the cache will also be encrypted on the iPhone."

This case is notable for several reasons:

- Apple made the decision to leak information containing personal identifiers—the names of all the observed WiFi networks in an area—in order to optimize the location calculations. By contrast, Google, which operates a similar service for Android phones, chose to go a different route that better preserved privacy: rather than send individual phones portions of its crowd-sourced databases, each phone sent Google the list of networks it was currently seeing, and Google would send back its server-calculated location based on that data. The result is the same —the current location of the phone—but Google's architecture didn't leak information collected by other phones.

---

2 Allan, Alasdair. "Got an IPhone or 3G IPad? Apple Is Recording Your Moves" (*http://bit.ly/radar-apple-loc*). OReilly Radar. April 20, 2011.

3 "Apple Q&A on Location Data" (*http://bit.ly/apple-loc-qa*). Apple Press Info. April 27, 2011.

While it's true that SSID information is broadcast in the clear and, as such, could be considered public information, the Apple model leaked *historical* information about WiFi networks. Anyone in range can see a WiFi network when it's turned on, but the Apple model made any network *ever observed in that area* available to any phone that visited that area, and in a larger area than the phone's radios could actually pick up. The result was that any visit to a geographical location with an iPhone was enough to retrieve wide-area wireless survey data as crowd-sourced and recorded by Apple.

- Apple's architectural decision to cache the data on the phone, along with a software bug that made that cached data persistent rather than transient as originally intended, inadvertently created a location-tracking database on the phone. This collection of cached information created a privacy risk for the phone owner.

In this case, Apple failed to properly minimize the data that lived on the phone, and created a system where the collection and storage of data was disproportionate to the ultimate need for it. In addition, Apple failed to secure that information from easy unauthorized access, thereby creating the risk of exposure of highly sensitive information about the movement of its customers.

Conclusion

The examples above illustrate how privacy protections can be thwarted from within, simply through small lapses in data-collection practices. However, there are myriad ways for external attackers to compromise your data and threaten its privacy. Systems designed with privacy and security in their architecture from the very beginning have a much better chance of protecting and upholding these values.

CHAPTER 4

Information Security: Protecting Data from Unauthorized Access

For the purposes of this book, privacy protection is primarily about regulating authorized access to and use of data. Information security (*InfoSec* for short, or cyber-security), which is primarily about stopping unauthorized access to information, is what makes privacy protection possible. Without controlling unauthorized access, building a privacy protection regime for authorized users is moot because any protection that can be easily circumvented is no true protection at all.

Whereas the implementation of privacy and security are concerned with guarding against different threats, they do make use of the same technologies such as encryption, auditing, logging, access controls, separation of concerns, alerting, active monitoring, and investigation. It could therefore be quite understandable for an organization that has not thought extensively about the underlying distinctions to mistake privacy for security. But an architecture is an arrangement of things to constitute a whole with desired properties, and the desired properties for protecting privacy and for securing against unauthorized access are not the same. Each requires unique design considerations.

If your organization does not have a dedicated information security team, get one. If your organization already has a dedicated InfoSec team, bring them into the design process early. As the experts on your network security, they will have invaluable advice on building a system that meets the security and compliance requirements for your organization.

Security requirements can have a huge impact on every aspect of system design. Data architecture, the ability of services to be co-located on the same machine, system performance, and even hardware budgets can be significantly affected by security requirements. If you wait until the end of designing your architecture to bring your

InfoSec team into the discussion, you may find yourself throwing out large parts of your design to meet security needs you forgot to consider.

InfoSec Best Practices for Privacy-Protected Systems

There are several high-level information security best practices that every enterprise should adopt. The technical details of implementing these are further documented elsewhere, and it's worth considering them in your designs.

Encrypting network traffic inside the system

Encrypting network traffic ensures that data cannot be intercepted by an attacker who is snooping on network traffic. As of 2014, the use of encryption to protect network traffic traveling over the open Internet is widespread, usually in the form of SSL/TLS connections. But inside data centers, server-to-server communications are often not encrypted. An attacker that gains access to such a network, even without access to the servers holding the data themselves, could still intercept privacy-protected data in transit between servers in a multi-machine cluster. Additionally, organizations are increasingly recording and analyzing their own network traffic to detect network intrusions. As a result, full copies of network traffic may be stored for long periods of time in these monitoring systems. This could lead to an inadvertent leak of privacy-protected data into a system that does not implement the same levels of control and oversight.

It's important for all network links that move privacy-protected data to use encryption. This applies not only to connections made by authorized users to access the system from outside the data center but also to network links between nodes in a multi-server system. In practice, this almost always requires an SSL/TLS or similar VPN layer between the users and the system. Inside the system itself, communications can be secured using SSL/TLS, IPSec, or some other point-to-point VPN technology.

Encryption-at-rest

Encryption-at-rest ensures that data is not stored as plain text. With this technique, as data is written to disk (or solid state drive, or tape, etc.), it is encrypted using a set of secret keys known only to privileged administrators of the system. This technique not only guards against data being compromised in a system breach where an attacker gains remote access to the storage system, but also against physical theft where the actual data-storage devices are stolen for later data extraction.

Encryption-at-rest can complicate system management, as the secret keys need to be supplied by a person at system startup and restart, rather than allowing for fully automated cycling of the system. Encryption-at-rest also requires careful auditing of all places where the data might be temporarily stored, such as temporary storage or caching servers.

Two-factor authentication

As its name suggests, two-factor authentication requires two pieces of information to be presented by a user before access to the system is granted. This makes compromising a legitimate user's account much more difficult that just figuring out their password.

While the first factor is usually a password, the second factor is typically a one-time passcode supplied by a specialized piece of hardware or software such as an RSA SecurID token or a smartphone application that performs the same function (like Google Authenticator or Duo Security). It could also be a one-time passcode supplied via an out-of-band communication mechanism such as an SMS text message or an automated phone call.

Though this makes authentication a bit more cumbersome, it forces any would-be attacker to not only compromise the user's password but also a physical device that is under their control. For even further security, three-factor authentication can follow up on every successful login with an email or SMS message so that a user can quickly be alerted of unauthorized account access and report it immediately.

Further Reading

If you're interested in learning more about the field of information security and some of the topics above, here are a few resources worth checking out:

Secrets & Lies (https://www.schneier.com/book-sandl.html)

Bruce Schneier's book lays out the proper framework for thinking about security: understanding how security technology works and how it fails, understanding the mindset of attackers, and how to look at security as a risk mitigation problem rather than a pass/fail challenge. His free monthly newsletter, *Crypto-Gram* (*http://bit.ly/crypto-gram*), is an excellent resource for interesting and notable news covering security research, technology, policy, and incident reports.

"How to Break into Security" (http://bit.ly/krebs-security)

Brian Krebs is a security researcher and prolific blogger. He recently interviewed several experts in the InfoSec world and published their advice on learning more about the profession and practice.

SANS Institute (http://www.sans.org/about/)

SANS offers training in the practice of information security and cyber defense. They also publish high-quality guides (*http://www.sans.org/security-resources/*) on different aspects of information security.

Open Web Application Security Project (OWASP) (http://bit.ly/owasp-cheat-sheet)
> For more on encryption within a system, the OWASP has published some extensive guidelines on securing the transport and network layers.

Guide to Storage Encryption Technologies for End User Devices (http://bit.ly/nist-encryption)
> The National Institute of Standards and Technology (NIST) has more exhaustive information on encryption-at-rest. In addition, most modern operating systems natively support encrypted disks, so your vendor documentation might not be a bad starting place.

Electronic Authentication Guideline (http://bit.ly/nist-ea-guideline)
> The NIST also provides more useful information on two-factor (and even three-factor) authentication.

Conclusion

You should now have a solid grasp of some of the main technical and legal themes at work in the privacy sphere. Within this context, sound data collection and information security practices are necessary foundations upon which to build specific privacy controls. By understanding your data, you can understand the forces at work upon it and how to protect it accordingly. In the next section, we'll dig into the many ways to design and control authorized access points to data.

PART II

Access and Control: Controlling Authorized Data Access

We have grouped our privacy-protective capabilities under two broad umbrellas—access and oversight. In this section, we discuss architectural choices related to data access. Access refers to the ability of users to see, share, and manipulate data within a system. The more precisely you can control access and the more nuanced those control decisions can be, the more flexibility your users have in finding ways to work with data within the FIPPs paradigm. A data-processing technology will generally function within a larger IT system that in itself must be secure as discussed in Chapter 5 on Security Architecture. Chapters 6 and 7 then explore the myriad possibilities for privacy protection offered by application-level access controls. As we'll show, these can be configured to do far more than just provide all-or-nothing access to data.

Security Architecture

Overview

Privacy and the potential violations thereof are intrinsic to our everyday notions of trust. When customers and citizens entrust private companies, NGOs, and government agencies with sensitive data, they would like to be assured that those organizations can and will handle it responsibly. In turn, organizations that serve as stewards of sensitive data must trust in their own people accordingly, often in new and uncharted ways. But sometimes people are untrustworthy—occasionally because of malicious intent, but more often because of honest mistakes and accidental errors. It's therefore imperative to become familiar with various ways to design technical methods that minimize the risk of having a class of users who must be trusted—of their own volition—to behave within a set of rules in order to safeguard privacy. A thorough security architecture will help you avoid creating a single point of trust in your systems.

Separating Roles, Separating Powers

Privacy controls serve to limit the behavior of users *inside* the system. However, to protect data from access occurring beyond the confines of the privacy-protected application (but rather at some lower system level), it's important to strictly separate the roles of individuals interacting with the system.[1] It's then possible to establish a clear separation of powers between these different roles.

---

1 This approach is sometimes also referred to as *separation of duties*.

Generally, an effective privacy-protection regime should account for the following five roles:

- The *end user*, who uses the software, either outside or within the data-stewarding organization
- The *application administrator*, responsible for the user-facing software's system maintenance—including data and users
- The *system administrator*, responsible for the operating system (e.g., Linux, Windows) and other components on which the application depends
- The *hardware or cloud administrator*, responsible for the upkeep and maintenance of the physical and/or virtual machines on which the software runs
- The *network administrator*, responsible for the secure operations of the organization's data-transfer systems

To properly separate roles, a few guidelines are necessary:

- Access controls must be used to refine what areas of the system users at each level can affect—both up and down the stack. For example, an end user should not be able to log in to one of the servers as a system-level user, and a system administrator must not be able to read application data. This method operates in contrast to the most common security architecture, in which each escalating level expands on the privileges of the level below. Rather, we recommend that each role should have its own disjoint set of allowed access.
- Each role's access to its own area must be through a technical intermediary that tracks user actions. In practice, this means that system administrators, for instance, would not be able to have raw shell access to machines and would instead use a management framework like Puppet (*https://puppetlabs.com*) or Chef (*https://www.chef.io/chef*) to create auditable changes to the machines.
- The systems that hold the logs recording the actions taken by users in each role must not be under that role's control.

This approach effectively solves the "who watches the watchers" conundrum by creating overlapping areas of concern and oversight at each layer boundary.

A typical set of checks that can result from a separation of roles might look like the following: the end user can be checked by the application administrator, the application administrator can be checked by the system administrator, and the system administrator and hardware administrator are unable to view data. The application administrator would be the only administrator who can view data inside the system, giving them a degree of control not shared by the other two administrators. In turn, an insider threat or information assurance team would be responsible for policing all of these roles without having direct access to the hardware, systems, application, or data. Each monitor would receive appropriate alerts when the action of a user in another role trips a threshold that indicates potential abuse.

Separating roles, conveniently, also functionally maps to a system architecture with access control points that log audit trails on every user action. At these crucial monitoring points, it's possible to automate many system tasks (thereby avoiding the risk of human error or malice), apply server-side access controls to data, and reserve direct system access for genuine emergencies.[2] Limiting direct root access is an important step to reducing risk, because it is often very difficult to audit such access, and root access can enable the gravest system vulnerabilities.

However, even in this most risk-laden of roles, it is sometimes still possible to detect behavior that indicates a malicious user trying to hide evidence of tampering. These techniques can be applied to those who administer and maintain system components, be they application, system, or hardware administrators. The practice of logging system events, discussed more thoroughly in Chapter 9, can extend to keeping a machine-readable history and lineage of all changes made to every piece of data over time. This allows your team to track how data is used, enabling you to properly specify known patterns or train algorithms for detecting abuse. Keeping tamper-resistant or tamper-evident trails of audit logs on every user action also can contribute to analysis, and help detect and deter privacy violations or other malicious or unintentionally damaging acts.

By keeping data on the server side, organizations can establish and enforce sound technical protections for privacy while still making data available through client applications that read and analyze (but do not allow bulk export of) data held on the servers. It's standard practice to limit data access to different users based on what they need in order to do their work and refrain from giving them direct or complete access to database servers.

Once data has been copied from a server to a local hard disk, the risk of undetected abuse increases because the stored information is now only controlled by policy and trust, not technical safeguards. It's therefore usually wise to prohibit users from downloading and saving data to their local machines. When data does need to be shared, it should be done from server to server. This assists in tagging changes and tracking source information, which in turn informs audit trails.

---

2 Access controls can be applied either at the level of enterprise servers or on individual users' client machines. Holding and applying access control policies on the server side makes it much more challenging for a user to compromise them. Users will be able to view relevant data held on the server, but they will not make or hold a local copy of the data on their own client machine. In contrast, if access controls are applied on the user's machine directly, the user will have a copy of the data and will be able to transfer that data elsewhere, either by uploading it to an external server or by copying it to external media that can be taken beyond your organization's control.

Making Roles Secure

Since each role should have different powers, it follows that each requires different methods to be made secure. Various controls can be applied in conjunction with regular oversight of alerts and subsequent investigation by your anti-abuse team.

The End User

To secure the end-user role, it is important to apply controls at the application level that lie outside the user's control. Beyond straight access controls, an organization might also set additional controls that govern the use of the system, such as those that include rate-limiting actions, setting limits on bulk downloads, or restricting export permissions. Such controls can prevent a user from, say, downloading 10,000 documents in 10 seconds. At the very least, if a user were to download 10,000 documents in 10 seconds, controls could trigger an alert to an insider threat team.

Figure 5-1 illustrates a simplified view of a system architecture for privacy-protected operations. End users access the data they need in the database and filesystem. Their access is mediated by the firewall-protected application server, which enforces the access controls on the underlying data and creates audit trails for each user operation. This audit data is sent to a second application server and data store that is used by the various audit and oversight teams to review the users' actions.

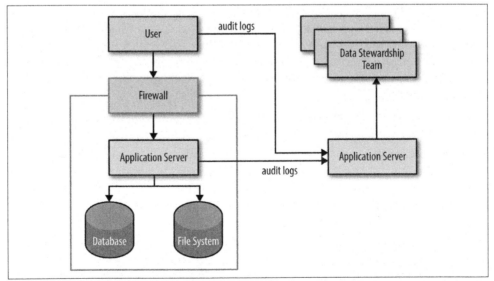

Figure 5-1. With access rules, export controls, and rate limiting on the server, users can access the limited subset of files relevant to their work, and no more.

While it may seem obvious, it's important to stress that all access controls must be applied on the server side. Sending data to the client, and trusting that code running there will adequately enforce policies surrounding which data can be seen, presents far more opportunities for security breaches. Only send to the client data that the user has access to.

Similarly, a system outside the end user's control must be used to record activity logs for later auditing. An anti-abuse team would then be responsible for actively reviewing those logs. With audit logs, application-level controls, and active oversight securing the end user's behavior, it becomes possible to significantly reduce the risk of bulk access or unauthorized disclosure. Additional controls can also be set and enforced on the user's computer. For more on audit logging, see Chapter 9.

The Application Administrator

It's important to monitor the application administrator, who has significant power because he or she needs to understand what data is in the system. Traditionally, this role is given login access to view all data inside the system. The application administrator may also frequently be given system tools access to address problems, filesystem access to transfer data, and database access to debug software and other system and data-integrity issues. In addition, they might have access to audit-log data. Consequently, a rogue administrator could theoretically turn off application server audit logs, log in as an end user, and then exfiltrate data. She could also deploy malicious code if the architecture allows plugins and extensions to be added to the system.[3]

To protect against these risks, organizations can use a standard technique to deny the administrator direct access to servers. Connections instead must pass through a host maintained by a third party, commonly called a *jumphost*. While connections to and from the jumphost are encrypted, the jumphost itself can peer into the commands as they traverse the system, creating a single point of monitoring to record all application administrator behavior that might take place outside of the audit logs recorded by the application itself. An insider threat team—perhaps part of the overall information security organization or a dedicated audit team specifically for this system— would then be responsible for actively reviewing those audit logs.

Figure 5-2 illustrates the use of a jumphost to monitor the actions of an application administrator. The jumphost produces audit data that is sent over to the systems used by the insider threat team.

---

3 Whereas textual commands can be audited, at the time of writing, binaries cannot be audited in any practical way.

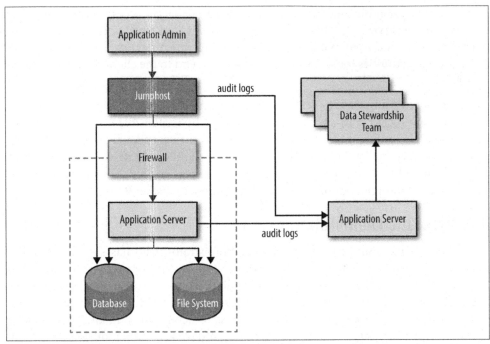

Figure 5-2. Application administrators' risk profile can be balanced by preventing direct access and auditing actions in a third-party system.

This process can even be made transparent to the application administrator through careful configuration of the jumphost. By preventing the administrator from altering or deleting the audit log of his or her actions, organizations can review the administrator's actions without requiring synchronized two-person review, a policy that is sometimes cumbersome to implement but often the only option for monitoring the behavior of someone who has root access to the system, as application administrators frequently do.

Since audit logs can be made machine-readable, organizations can also apply rules to detect suspicious behavior patterns and take action in real time, as discussed in Chapter 9. Organizations can also review the audit logs to identify potential areas of risk based on the administrator's past actions. The insider threat team would be responsible for conducting this type of continuous monitoring and analysis.

Protecting against malicious code deployment is more difficult. Organizations may consider requiring reviews of all code written by insiders in order to prevent the application administrator from deploying malicious code. If implemented, the code review process should be conducted in small batches to improve the quality of review. In a secure code deployment pipeline, the application administrator should check the source code into a repository that is then reviewed by a second developer. The code should then be compiled and signed by an automated build system outside of the developer's control. The system administrator should then enforce a check at the application-server level that only permits signed binaries to be deployed. This step prevents the application administrator from deploying code outside the review process.[4]

The System Administrator

It's common practice for system administrators to have root or "superuser" access to the operating system—allowing them to alter any part of the system in ways that are difficult to detect. This presents risks because the system administrator can turn off or cripple functions in undetectable ways, and enforcing controls at the system level against any superuser is clearly ineffective. Instead, the most effective way to audit system administrator behavior is proxy-shell access through jumphosts, as discussed above. Using a jumphost will record all the behavior of the system administrator as a series of issued shell commands.

However, while auditing the shell commands issued by the superuser is theoretically effective, it presents some challenges. First, given the free-form nature of command-line administration, it requires someone with system administrator-level knowledge to decode what the commands mean. Second, even when the commands themselves are clear, decoding what the effect of any given shell command is can sometimes be very difficult to do—even for another system administrator—without painstakingly reconstructing the state of the system at the time the shell command was run. Finally, given that command shells are effectively programming languages, it is easy to carefully obfuscate the true meaning of a sequence of commands, effectively making automation useless in detecting malicious behavior.

Because of all this, in a production system with sensitive data, superuser access to a live production server should be reserved for emergencies. The easiest way to do this is by implementing automated system configuration management, which requires system edits in more or less the same way that source code is controlled. To be deployed against a server containing sensitive data, commands should be written into a script, reviewed by another administrator, and automatically deployed once approved.

These technical and procedural steps, illustrated in Figure 5-3, prevent any single administrator from inserting commands directly into a production system as the superuser. These techniques for command scripting and review have become standard engineering practice for companies practicing cloud deployment. In some cases,

---

4 See Jez Humble & David Farley, *Continuous Delivery: Reliable Software Releases through Build, Test, and Deployment Automation (http://continuousdelivery.com/)* (Addison-Wesley, 2010).

emergency access may be necessary, but these contingencies are rare, discrete, and easily monitored. In other words, manual access should only be granted in highly-controlled special cases and not during normal business operations.

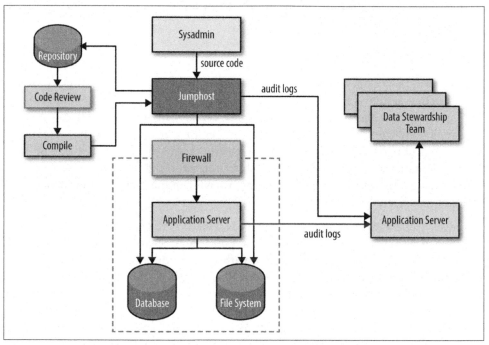

Figure 5-3. Sysadmins make changes only after their instructions are reviewed and deployed like software code. This is becoming more and more common in enterprise cloud setups.

In addition, data should be encrypted at rest, and the keys should be held by the application administrator. If data is encrypted at the application level, then the system administrator should have no access without superuser permissions. And even when encryption is performed at the system level, the system administrator should still not have access to the encryption keys required to start up the protected machines.

This brings us to secure key management. When encrypting data at rest, the encryption keys can either be stored on internal systems or be held externally using a hardware security module (HSM), a tamper-evident and tamper-resistant external device that securely generates and holds encryption keys. Modern server-based information-processing systems (including increasingly popular cloud-based offerings) tend to hold many encryption keys, which in turn are often secured and managed by a single master key. However, you'll want a secure way of managing all of your keys, because whether you store them on external hardware accessories or on internal systems, a compromised encryption key means substantially increased risks to privacy concerns around sensitive data that is no longer reliably secured.

The following is a generic example of a secure key management system, which is entirely automated and requires no manual entry or transfer of encryption keys.

A master key management system generates, encrypts, stores, and backs up a master key in conjunction with an HSM. The master key manager service communicates with client key management systems that assist in running other independent software on various servers. The client key managers obtain key material from the master key manager. In addition, the client key managers regularly report their status to the master key manager. The master key manager in turn monitors their behavior for anything irregular or suspicious. The master key manager tracks various timeout periods on the master keys as well as on the client key managers and their subcomponents. If a client key manager exceeds the time limit for reporting in as scheduled, or begins communication unexpectedly early, the master key manager will stop trusting it and will not provide it with keys. When a client key manager needs an encryption key (e.g., to mount an encrypted volume or access encrypted data), it asks the master key manager. After the master key manager verifies that the client key manager isn't raising any security flags, it sends the encrypted key to the HSM, which then decrypts the key and sends it back. It is only at this point that the master key manager provides the appropriate unencrypted key to the client key manager.

This type of a key management setup would provide an additional check on internal and external threats such as rogue system administrators or cloud administrators: if you decide you want to sever your relationship with them, the HSM and master key manager give you the option of destroying the master key and shutting down all the connected client key managers, thus rendering all the data you entrusted to that third party inaccessible.

The Hardware or Cloud Administrator

The hardware administrator has physical access to the machines. This role presents risks because hardware administrators can copy and steal hard drives or insert malicious hardware, either of which could result in compromised data. Organizations can limit this risk by employing encryption of data at rest, as described above and in Chapter 4, and taking physical security steps. For instance, at most commercial data centers or cloud-computing services, hardware devices are separated and locked in physical cages. There are many other steps, such as using sensors, locking hardware, and auditing, that can further secure this process.

A Note on Cloud Architectures

Many modern systems are built on top of cloud infrastructure, where data systems and servers are actually virtualized software constructs running on top of a managed hardware infrastructure whose details are opaque to the end user. Even if each role in the stack we describe is not inside your organization, it is usually still possible to get the details of each employee role's access level at the cloud provider, under what circumstances they can access customer data, what logging and auditing is in place around those actions, and what you can expect in terms of disclosure when these privileged accesses take place. Contact your cloud provider and get detailed (and contractual) descriptions of these details, and let them inform the rest of your security design.

For example, a cloud-hosting provider that allows its administrators to inspect file systems but does not record auditing data for these actions might require you to perform full-disk encryption on your cloud volumes. Assuming that the encryption keys will be provided over a virtual serial console on boot, this strategy would be sound as long as any access to serial console streams by provider staff is logged and audited.

However, the most important step in enforcing adequate physical security is to maintain the proper separation of roles. In a large data center, a hardware administrator should be unaware of the details of the systems he or she is administering. Not knowing which is which, the hardware administrator should instead respond to requests at the level of the server rack and the machine. Sometimes, the hardware administrator role is not carefully separated from others, and some data centers do not control access other than at the border of the facility. Such an approach disproportionately relies on trust rather than technology and verification, and is not recommended. Instead, care should be taken in selecting data centers that are conscientious about the subtleties of protecting their customers' sensitive data.

The Network Administrator

Another role, overlapping in some cases with some of the responsibilities of the system administrator or the hardware administrator, is the person who administers an organization's networks. The network administrator operates at one layer of architectural abstraction away from individual systems where data is held and processed; it's a role that serves as the gateway to the machines but doesn't actually touch the content of those machines. The network administrator is responsible for authorizing and maintaining LAN, WAN, and VPN access; monitoring incoming and outgoing traffic across networks and between machines on the organization's intranet; assigning and managing IP addresses; administering firewalls and whitelists; testing for network security weaknesses; and keeping security tracking regimes up-to-date.

In short, the network administrator is involved in managing internal and external risks, focusing primarily on the latter. The network administrator ensures that the initial lines of defense are in place to prevent undesired network traffic and closes gateways through which an attacker could assault the organization's machines.

To that end, network administrators also capture and analyze ("sniff") network traffic to determine if malicious actors are monitoring communications over the network. Because of this, we recommend that internal traffic between machines be encrypted to mitigate the risks posed by external snooping and rogue network administrators. To further minimize the risks a network administrator might pose, an organization should allow only encrypted access to its sensitive applications and those applications' internal communications. Network administrators should also not be granted the power to generate new SSL certificates, which they could use to spoof connections. These steps will substantially reduce their threat profile.

In much the same way that encryption-at-rest limits the damage that someone with access to the hardware can do, encryption-in-flight limits the damage that someone who owns the network can inflict. A network administrator could still execute denial-of-service (DOS) attacks, but these do not represent a privacy risk on a technical level. As part of our recommended loop-of-oversight, an organization's network information security team (the ultimate monitors) should watch the network administrators, examining system monitoring data and not any raw content.

Conclusion

Separating powers and roles is a traditional mechanism to implement the well-known principle of checks and balances. Different factions in different roles enforce controls against each other such that no faction or single individual can engage in abuse without detection. When properly executed in information-processing systems, such an approach can provide substantial structural improvements to safeguarding privacy. Such a separation of roles inherently creates a framework of oversight, one predicated on carefully controlled access to systems and data.

CHAPTER 6

Access Controls

Overview

Access controls are a crucial layer of data management and security. By "access controls," we mean any electronic mechanisms designed to limit the availability of data to users *within* an application. (Electronic mechanisms that limit access to the application itself, such as a login and password, would fall under information security, discussed in Chapter 4.)

Of all the capabilities discussed in this book, access controls may be the most malleable in terms of supporting diverse privacy requirements. Numerous aspects of an enterprise's privacy policy will rely on access controls as a means of ensuring proportionality in data access, controlling data usage, and enhancing security beyond the broad system-access level. Access controls are quite versatile—there are ways to control access to the information itself (access control models), and ways to control what you can do to the information once you have access to it (access types). Access controls can even be used to limit the knowledge of the data's existence—separate from the contents of the data. This hiding of the existence of a record can be an important part of safeguarding privacy.

The more precisely access controls can be defined and the more flexibly they can be applied, the more policy options that become available to those trying to create a robust privacy-protective regime around the use of the technology. Such flexibility reduces friction with the technology and supports creative innovation.

Keep in mind that when we refer to a *system*, we're speaking about the overarching, coherent data system, which will likely be composed of multiple servers responsible for different aspects of functionality. The realization of some of the access control patterns we describe will probably require interlocking pieces of functionality running on multiple, logical (i.e., virtual or corporeal) computer systems.

Access-Control Models

Potential use cases for an application may involve the use of the same core data in a variety of contexts and by multiple people fulfilling various roles in an organization. An effective, flexible security environment, then, must allow many users to have multiple and varying access permissions in order to utilize data with multiple and varying access restrictions. There is no single ideal configuration for this security environment. For example, small organizations with a limited number of users who access data for the same general purpose may only need a few basic access control options because users are authorized to see broad cuts of the data. But larger organizations with a significant number of users each accessing data for a wide variety of purposes will likely need greater diversity of access-control options. Selecting the right one will depend on the specific context in which the system will operate. System designers can choose between several levels of access control granularity:

Network/system-level security

> Users in this configuration are given broad access to the data in a system. They can access either an entire network of databases or the entirety of a single database.[1] You can envision this as the electronic equivalent of a large filing cabinet with a single lock on it. When the single lock is opened, the entire contents of the filing cabinet are available.

Collection-level security

> Data within the system is maintained in various distinct data structures, such as database tables. Users can access an entire, coherent collection of information within the larger data system but be restricted from others. In this case, each drawer in our filing cabinet has a separate lock with different users having different sets of keys. Once they open the drawers, they have access to all the file folders and their contents within that drawer.

Record-level security

> Users are restricted from accessing information on a record-by-record basis. In this case, our filing cabinet metaphor starts to become insufficient, but imagine that once a user has opened the file drawer there were some means of controlling which folders the user could open, at which point the user would be able to view all of the documents within that folder.

Cell-level security

> In this configuration, access is controlled on a data-point-by-data-point basis. For each level of granularity of chopped-up data in your system, there is a sepa-

---

[1] Generally, this will be done through a basic login and password, at which point all data in the system will be available to them. In this case, there are no additional access-control mechanisms—the access control is synonymous with the system login. We include it here for the sake of completeness.

rate access control for that discrete segment of information. By now, our metaphor has all but fled the field, but you could think of this as some means of redacting the documents within the folder on a page-by-page basis depending on each user's authorization.

Sub-cell-level security

Here, you are not only controlling access to the data in your database but also data about the data (the metadata). Metadata may include information about the time and date of the creation of the data in the system, the system user who originally input the data, previous modifications of the data, and other information relevant to the creation and use of the data. At this point, our metaphor is in tatters. One way to understand this would be to imagine a separate filing cabinet next to our original filing cabinet, where the new filing cabinet has all of the aforementioned data about the first filing cabinet stored with its own cell-level access controls.

However, not all systems will need controls as granular as sub-cell level security. Each of the levels above can be optimal in the right context. Selecting the right level of granularity for a specific application will depend on the situation, and a few considerations can help you determine the appropriate level. For instance:

- How big is the system in terms of both users and data? The more users and the more data in the system, the more likely the system will contain data not every user needs to see.

- Will some or all of those users have different uses for the system? A system with a single purpose will likely require fewer access controls because everyone who logs in to the system will probably need to see the same data. More complex systems involving a wider variety of data used for a greater array of purposes are likely to have more complex access requirements.

- Can the data be structured in a way that lends itself to logical divisions? The level of granularity necessarily depends on how small you can chunk the data while still being sensible to the user. If the data is only understandable when viewed at the record-level, then it would be useless to enable access control at the cell level. This would be like allowing a system to secure words one letter at a time—it's hard to find the point of securing every other letter in a w_r_, for example.

These factors will all interact to help determine the right level of access control. Consider the following examples:

Electronic library card-catalog system

Many users may access the system, but generally, all are using the system for the same purpose—to find books. The data looks like the standard card catalog information, with a row of the database table representing a single index card where each cell in that row contains information such as title, author, ISBN, Dewey decimal system number, etc. In this case, there might be little need for a very granular access control regime, as libraries typically do not deny people access to portions of the card catalog. However, perhaps the library has a separate children's/young adult catalog (as often is the case), and the library would rather not have minors browsing some of the racier titles on its shelves. In this case, it might opt for table-level security, where one table contains children's titles, and the other, adult titles. The library is unlikely to require cell-level security, however, because there is usually not any reason to obscure portions of a library index card.

Alternatively, using a record-level approach, the same library could structure its card catalog as a single table of cards and restrict access to just the racier titles in the library (assuming they are marked accordingly). This would allow young adults free reign of the whole library, minus some select works of Henry Miller. While the record-level security requires greater granularity in marking individual records than the two catalogs approach, it maximizes the ability of any patron, regardless of age, to access as much of the library as possible—something that is probably core to the mission of the library.

Health clinic patient-record system

A limited number of nurses and physicians in a clinic might end up treating any patient who walks in the door. In a greatly simplified version of an electronic medical record (EMR) system, let's say a patient record is contained in a single row in a database table with each cell containing various bits of information such as contact information, prior conditions, notes on the diagnoses, tests performed, drugs prescribed, and so on. If the system is only accessed by the doctors and nurses to manage patient records, then system- or collection-level security would be sufficient. However, suppose the system is also used to manage patient billing. Now billing clerks also require access to the system. They might need to see the list of tests performed as well as basic patient contact information, but they would not need to see other information in the record, such as potentially sensitive patient history. In this scenario, cell-level security might be more privacy-protective because it would allow the clerks to have access to only those portions of the patient record necessary to do their jobs. Figure 6-1 illustrates alternative views of an EMR using cell-level security.

Intelligence analysis system

Consider a massive database, one that might be used by a national government intelligence agency. Data comes from a variety of sources, including highly-protected operational assets (i.e., spies) or sophisticated and secret electronic-collection methods. The collected data may be used by potentially hundreds or even thousands of analysts for a variety of purposes—counter-terrorism, detection of economic espionage, defense of electronic networks, counter-intelligence, support for foreign policy initiatives, etc. Operational security is very high and includes multiple security clearance classifications that must be attached to the data. In addition, there is a high level of public demand for protection of individual privacy. This should lead to policies designed to minimize exposure of data to only those analysts with an absolute need to view it (and official authorization to see the information). Here, sub-cell level security is best suited to provide the flexibility essential to managing this complex spider web of security needs. Securing data on a point-by-point basis allows administrators to carefully control the potential exposure of information. In addition, separately securing the metadata also ensures that critical information about the data remains available to those who need it while safeguarding potentially sensitive details from other users (e.g., information about a data source or the system user who created it might reveal closely-held details about a particular source or method of collection).

Doctor's View of EMR

Name	Address	Patient History	Tests Performed	Diagnosis	Drugs Prescribed	Insurance Provider	Credit Card Information
John Doe	123 Main Street, USA	Chronic flatulence	Hit knee with little hammer	Knee pain	Morphine		

Billing Clerk's View of EMR

Name	Address	Patient History	Tests Performed	Diagnosis	Drugs Prescribed	Insurance Provider	Credit Card Information
John Doe	123 Main Street, USA		Hit knee with little hammer			Very Good Insurance, Inc.	Visa

Figure 6-1. Cell-level security reveals only the information necessary to support a particular user's needs.

While these examples are fairly notional, they serve to highlight the balance that must be struck between *effectiveness*—a system delivering its intended utility for its users—and *privacy*. Questions of which type of access control method to implement may also be constrained (or at least made more difficult) by what is technically and administratively feasible, given that access controls often rely on good metadata with which to make decisions. Properly tagging whole data sets with useful metadata can be a very tough organizational challenge.

When designing a new system, it's important to preserve flexibility for future decisions that would require finer-grained access control than currently in place. For example, if you build in mechanisms that can enable sub-cell access controls from the start, then you will never have to sacrifice more granular access controls in the future as a result of technical decisions made before their requirement arose.

Types of Access

The most basic access control system is binary—either a user has total control over a set of data or a user has absolutely no control over that data (and may not even be aware of its existence). The user can see and edit a patient record or an intelligence report, or the user cannot.

However, as noted above, the more flexibility available within a system, the more likely it can be tailored precisely to maximize privacy protection *and* effectively accomplish whatever purposes it has been designed to achieve. Some users may only be able to see data. Others might be able to control every aspect of the data, including granting access to others. Still others may only be granted limited awareness of the data they are seeking. A system that allows a variety of types of access increases configuration options by allowing degrees of control over data.

Basic Access

At a minimum, an access control system will rely on four basic types of access to data:

No access
> A user cannot see the data at all. Sometimes, there is not even an indication that the data exists in the system. If the user types "John Doe" into the search field, the system will return no results even if "John Doe" is in the system.[2]

> While "no access" may seem like a straightforward concept to implement, it's trickier than it may first appear. There are numerous pitfalls that involve accidentally leaking the existence of information without leaking the information itself. For example, imagine a record made up of ten cells, two of them restricted as "no access" to a set of users. If the routine that calculates the summary of the record does not take the access controls into account, it may report to users that there are ten cells that make up this record while only showing eight—effectively leaking to the user that there are two cells of the record that are hidden to their level of access. Similarly, a user may see the name of a database table in a listing of tables that they cannot read rows from.

> In a "no access" scenario, it's important to think carefully about whether just the data, or the fact of its existence (or even potential to exist), needs to be hidden from certain users.

---

2 We're using simple searches as examples here, but these access types can be applied to any means of retrieving information in the system.

Read access

> A user can view the data but cannot modify it. Typing "John Doe" into the search bar returns networks, databases, or records (depending on the granularity of the access control model implemented) containing the term "John Doe" and the user can view that information. However, the user cannot edit the information, nor can the user grant or deny access to the information to other users.

Write access

> Not only can a user view the data, but the user can also modify it. Typing "John Doe" into the search bar pulls up data concerning John Doe, and the user can add new information and save it to the system for other users to view.

Owner access

> A user has complete control of the data. The user can retrieve the data in the system, make modifications to it, delete the data, and grant or deny access to other users in the system.

Discovery Access

Beyond these basic access types, systems can be configured to offer even more nuanced access options. In some cases, data owners might want to allow users to know that information exists within a system without revealing specific details. This type of access can increase user confidence that they are more likely to find information relevant to their use of the system while preventing overbroad access.

A frequent argument against the use of rigid access controls is that they might prevent users from seeing information that could be vital to accomplishing their objectives. At the same time, it may not always be possible to determine immediately whether information is relevant or not. Such determinations might be context-specific to changing conditions such as user roles, real-world events, exigent circumstances, and other factors. Discovery access provides a mechanism to err on the side of privacy while slightly cracking the door open to access.

Discovery access can take a variety of forms. For example, a search for "John Doe" could return a message that information concerning John Doe does exist within the system but does not return the details of that actual John Doe data. Instead, a user might be able to access the John Doe record (a row in the database) where the user can see some of the data in that record (a selection of cells within the row) and also can see a message that more data (additional cells within the row) is available.[3] The message could also be configured to provide some indication as to the type of data made available. For example, it might tell the user, "There is more data available on John Doe: phone number, address, and medical records." Equipped with this infor-

---

3 This is only possible if the system is configured using the cell- or sub-cell-level security model.

mation, the user could then go to a system administrator or anyone in the system with "owner access" to the data and request access (generally, the message to the user would contain instructions, both administrative and technical, for how the user could obtain access to the data).

However, discovery access can also create some security risk by allowing users to draw potentially privacy-infringing inferences even from the limited information available. Take a very basic example: if a database contains a list of sex offenders and a user types "John Doe" and receives a message that a John Doe record is in the system, then an analyst can easily conclude that John Doe is a sex offender. This becomes potentially even more damaging if the database contains mixed information. For instance, if the aforementioned database contained both the names of sex offenders *and* their victims, then a search hit regarding John Doe might lead someone to erroneously conclude that John Doe is a sex offender when in fact he was a victim.

Discovery permissions are also vulnerable to more sophisticated attacks, particularly through the use of conjunctive searching. Imagine a database that contains medical records where someone wants to determine if a patient has a certain medical condition. If the attacker searched for "John Doe AND syphilis" and received a positive match, the user would then know that there was a record in the system containing both those terms together and draw a conclusion about John Doe's past or present medical condition. Some organizations choose to disable conjunctive searching for this reason. Others allow it but use careful auditing and oversight to find patterns of abusive conjunctive searching to guard against attacks.

These vulnerabilities should not discourage you from considering using discovery access in your access control design. Rather, you should carefully weigh the security risks and their potential consequences for data subjects against the overall benefit of more nuanced and controlled sharing decisions enabled by this permission.

Managing Access

On top of these building blocks of access, you can layer additional limitations designed to control who can see the data, when they can see the data, and what they can do with the data once they can see it.

Role-Based Access

Role-based access refers to access to data that is based on the characteristics of the individual user. These characteristics can involve such things as the user's position within an organization, their mission (i.e., what they do every day), or their level of security clearance. For commercial systems, these characteristics might be simply based on the subscription level of a customer paying for access to data. Once these characteristics are identified, users are organized into groupings called *access control lists* (ACLs). Each ACL is then granted one of the above types of access to a discrete set of data.

Role-based access regimes can be very basic or they can be as complex and granular as the access control model allows. Most systems will, at the very least, have an administrator ACL consisting of individuals with complete access to the data in the system, the ability to create new ACLs, and the ability to add or remove users from them as needed. Beyond that, there is no set standard for how to create ACLs, and the organization of your particular access control regime will largely depend on the context in which it is built (i.e., who your users are and the data they need to use).

For instance, imagine a cell-level security data system designed for a major metropolitan hospital. A variety of roles might be reflected in the organization of the ACLs. Some ACLs might be organized based on particular hospital departments—Oncology, Epidemiology, Cardiology, etc. Others might be built according to the organizational structure of the personnel—surgeons, nurses, pharmacists, lawyers, etc. The ACLs can be hierarchical, containing sub-ACLs such as Supervisors and General Users within each category. The following figure offers a sample map of such an access control regime.

Time-Based Access, or Data Leasing

Access controls can also be temporal in nature, allowing data stewards to share information for only a designated period of time. Temporal access controls give users access to the data for a predetermined time at the end of which the system automatically revokes the privileges. This type of "data leasing" encourages data sharing when circumstances require it, but provides assurances that access privileges will revert to the *status quo* once there is no longer a need, without any further action on the part of the data steward. This can be particularly useful in a large, complex access control regime where data stewards may already be overwhelmed by sizeable data management responsibilities.

Temporal access controls are generally best for circumstances where the access period is predetermined. For example, an employee is temporarily seconded to another department with new data access needs for 30 days. Of course, circumstances can change, so some systems might also use an automatic notification (such as a pop-up message on login or some kind of email alert) notifying a user that their access privileges are expiring. Such a notification could advise the employee to contact the data steward to request an extension of those privileges.

Temporal access controls can be applied either because of temporal factors related to the status of the person accessing the data (as above), or based on the temporal relevance of the data itself. For example, automated license plate reader (ALPR) data is very useful in tracking down stolen cars, but can be thought of as having a finite window of relevance—most stolen cars will be dumped, broken down piecemeal and sold for parts, or have their plates changed within a matter of days. Allowing investigators unfettered access to search a week's worth of data could greatly aid in those investigations while still preventing improper use of the larger collection of license plate records.

Functional Access

Functional access control applies not to access to the data in the system but to the system's functionality itself. Data analytics systems offer a variety of tools to the users, from basic capabilities like cutting and pasting text to sophisticated analytic capabilities specially designed to extract specific insights from a data set. Functional access controls allow administrators to control *how* users interact with the data to which they have access. Administrators concerned about exfiltration of important data might allow only certain, trusted users to utilize built-in data export or sharing features. In other cases, administrators might want to prevent selected users from accessing certain analytic tools that could lead to the revelation of particularly sensitive insights about a data subject that should not be available to those users.

Strengths and Weaknesses of Access Control

The assorted variations of access control can be combined in nearly infinite configurations in order to meet the specific requirements of a data system. Consequently, it can be difficult to evaluate their general effectiveness without a specific operational context. This section discusses the strengths and weaknesses of access controls in very general terms, and it's important to recognize that the relative degree of these strengths and weaknesses may vary considerably depending on the specific characteristics of the system in question.

Strengths

The primary strengths to consider are as follows:

Flexibility
> System architects have an almost overwhelming number of options when it comes to selecting the overarching access control model, generating the ACL membership rolls, and determining the type of access that each of those ACLs should have. Systems can secure data broadly through a few large ACLs, or they can be composed of thousands of different ACLs with painstakingly intricate access permissions attached to each data point in the system. Therefore, system architects will have multiple configuration options to choose from when attempting to design a system that meets both analytic and privacy imperatives.

Security

Access controls offer an additional layer of security beyond the initial user login to the system—just because someone has access to the system does not mean they can see everything in it. This allows the consolidation of more data within a single data system without necessarily exposing all of that data to every system user. Without internal access controls, it would be more difficult to build large data systems with a significant number of users without substantially increasing risks to privacy.

Control

The word speaks for itself. Access controls give data stewards far greater control over their data. They can precisely manage who can see data and how they can interact with it. Such control often encourages greater data sharing. Data owners can be more confident that when data is shared with users, they can be selective about these sharing decisions. Data owners can carefully limit user actions to those allowed by law and/or necessary to accomplish a specific function.

Dynamism

Access controls can be configured in ways that allow frequent changes to permissions depending on changing circumstances. Through temporal controls, conditional controls, and ad hoc decisions made by users with owner access, data access can be expanded or contracted in response to ever-changing technical, legal, and ethical imperatives. No access control regime has to be permanent, which allows data stewards to err on the side of privacy with the confidence that adjustments can be made as warranted.

Weaknesses

Following are a few weaknesses of access controls:

Scale

As systems scale both in terms of users and data, it can become increasingly difficult to maintain a granular access control regime. Managing millions of records within a cell-level or sub-cell-level security model would require a significant commitment of personnel and time in order to make effective data-management decisions. Without those resources, a data steward is more likely to grant broad access to users to ensure they have access to the data they need, thereby negating the potential privacy benefits of a granular regime tailored to specific needs. However, careful generation and capture of metadata that can automate the application of access controls can offset some of the undue burden of painstaking and error-prone manual administration of access control lists.

Ease of use

> Access control user interfaces are notoriously weak and often last on the list of priorities for user experience (UX) in software development. In order to make access control decisions effectively, a data steward must know, at the very least, the complete membership of an access control list as well as details about the complete set of data to which those lists are being granted access. This requires a user either to know this information already or somehow to be provided with this information when they begin to interact with the interface. If a data steward wants to allow ACL X, comprised of 100 system users, to see Database A, comprised of 100 records, how can they be provided the necessary feedback to clearly understand the implications of this decision? Are they fully cognizant that every user in ACL X needs to see every record in Database A? Not only do most user interfaces not provide the necessary feedback to give a user complete information, but any attempt to do so would quickly become unwieldy.

Dynamism

> This strength can also be a potential weakness. Allowing access controls to be adjustable to account for changing circumstances also means they can be changed for nefarious reasons. Consequently, an access control regime with any dynamism also makes data potentially vulnerable because it must rely to some extent on trust in those charged with responsibility for managing access decisions. Other capabilities, such as the oversight mechanisms discussed in Part III, can mitigate some of this vulnerability.

Access Controls and the Fair Information Practice Principles (FIPPs)

Access controls are enormously helpful in implementing each of the Fair Information Practice Principles:

Collection limitation

> Although access control itself is managed after collection, the architectural decisions implementing it do have an effect on how data is collected. Adopting a granular security model for your data allows more precise data collection decisions, enabling data stewards to manage only the exact data points necessary to accomplish a goal.

Data quality

> Careful control over who can access data and what those users can do with that data can help to maintain data quality by ensuring that only appropriately authorized and suitably trained users can make modifications or deletions.

Purpose specification/use limitation
> Access controls can be configured to provide data access only to those system users who will handle the data in accordance with the authorized purposes for which the data was collected.

Security safeguards
> Access controls provide additional layers of security for data beyond just general access to the system.

Accountability
> Access controls can be used to establish roles within the system based on the authorities and skills of the ACL members. Those with more access and more functional capabilities are held responsible for the management of the data under their purview.

When to Use Access Controls

Put simply: always use access controls.

Almost every system will have some sort of login and password (i.e., system-level security) in order to control who can use the system. Generally, any system with multiple users and more than 100 or so records will not need to share all data with every user. These systems might be able to operate within the letter of the law without access controls or with very basic access control regimes, but it's likely they will be sharing some data with users who do not need to see it to do their jobs. By more carefully controlling your data with sufficiently granular access controls, you create a system that can tailor data access exactly to data needs and therefore reduce any unnecessary infringement of privacy.

Further considerations will affect the specific structure of your access control regime. Several factors will influence your design decisions:

Data scale/granularity
> The numbe of data points in the system. This does not refer to the number of bytes of data in the system—a massive system could contain a few very large data files. Instead, this refers to the number of discrete pieces of information that could be consumed by a human user. For example, a record contains a person's name and a phone number. This record actually could contain up to seven (or more) data points that could be controlled—first name, middle name(s), last name, country code, area code, prefix, and line number.

Data schema
> The organization of the data itself. This might sit on a spectrum between a hierarchical structure (e.g., databases, records, data points, etc.) and a huge number of single data points with no order at all.

User scale
> The number of system users that will interact with the data.

System uses
> The potential applications of the system. A system could be designed to interact with data for a single use, or it could aggregate data and make it available for a nearly infinite variety of uses on the frontend.

Dynamism
> The potential for these and other factors to change over time. A static system might involve the same basic users, data, and functionality over a long period, whereas a dynamic system might involve constant flows of new data, new users, and new uses.

Support personnel
> The people who are charged with managing the data and the access control lists. This could range from a single person charged with multiple administrative tasks with little time and/or knowledge for access management to an elaborate regime of multiple data administrators solely tasked with managing system access.

These factors will play off of each other in a variety of ways. A system with a large number of data points, large user base, and dynamic data flows will need a large number of support personnel to manage the data at a granular level. If such infrastructure is not available, then you might want to go with a less granular access control regime. On the other hand, a static system with even a large number of users and data points might allow for a more granular regime if time can be initially invested to set a workable access control regime that rarely requires adjustment. Meanwhile, a small data set with a large number of users might only need a few basic data controls—the only data management investment would be putting users into appropriate ACLs.

As you can probably guess, the possibilities are as extensive as the number of combinations of the various types of access controls. It will be up to you as the system architect to design a system that maximizes data utility and privacy protection.

Conclusion

You can think of application-level security (as opposed to the system- and physical-level security of the machines themselves) as having two key aspects: restriction and oversight. Restriction allows the architect to build a system that enforces its own rules without human intervention. Oversight lets careful observations of the use of the system limit the abuse a user can inflict given the access that they have. Both are necessary and neither is sufficient to create truly robust privacy protections alone.

As such, ACLs play a huge role in creating a privacy-protected system as they are *the* mechanism for application-level restrictions. While intelligently implementing ACLs may seem complicated (and it is), they are half of the heart and soul of privacy protections in your software. As an architect, expect to spend a good deal of time on this aspect of your system.

Finally, while it's important to be careful and rigorous in the ACL regimes you create, ACLs can be thought of as a primitive functionality that is ripe for innovation. A fresh, usable-but-effective take on managing access control lists could spawn a new long-lasting paradigm in application design. Get creative.

CHAPTER 7

Data Revelation

Overview

Access controls provide a critical base for a robust privacy architecture by grounding the concept of a *right-to-know* (or authorized access to) information. But the qualified use of sensitive data must often rise to higher standards. These often entail a careful balancing of contextually determined requirements and limitations that reflect a user's *need-to-know*.

Selective, purpose-driven, and scope-driven revelation (collectively referred to as "data revelation" throughout the chapter) techniques provide a toolbox of practical measures for limiting retrieval and use of data in accordance with discrete, well-defined use cases and operational needs. These practices can provide clear conditions to justify refining and focusing the scope of information exposure and processing even more tightly than controls established by access privileges alone. Minimizing data exposure in this way can mitigate the risks (both perceived and actual) of privacy harms from over-broad disclosure and unwarranted repurposing of data. They constitute an integral part of privacy-protective systems architecture.

The Case for Data Revelation

In the era of ubiquitous data collection, plummeting capture and storage costs, and immense potential to create emergent privacy harms through the intermingling of disparate data sources,[1] there is an ever-increasing need to address privacy risks at the

---

[1] Orin Kerr on "mosaic theory" (*http://bit.ly/ssrn-kerr-mosaic*) describes the phenomena of data sources merged into information "mosaics" that present challenges to privacy of individuals in ways that singular data sources independently could not.

level of information processing and data exposure. Access controls go a long way in ensuring that specific data sources or classifications are restricted to authorized user groups; however, the sheer abundance of the data that can be governed by the corresponding access control groups may still far exceed the bounds of what is necessary to be disclosed or used in any given analytical context. Therefore, while access control methods specify a necessary baseline for access to types of data, those rigid permissions tend to be sufficient only in more simplified or idealized circumstances where access is extremely well-defined and consistent over time. In more realistic scenarios, access controls may be too coarse or static, and additional granularity and flexibility may be required when conditionally revealing data to users.

Over-exposure of data not only creates risks for the privacy of data subjects, but may also impede the ability of users to make sense or effective use of the information to which they have been granted access. Constraints that serve to narrow data exposure —even when the full scope of the data type or source falls within a more general authorization or right-to-know—can serve as valuable guardrails to help keep information usage on track by limiting the prospects of unwarranted inquiries. Just as overly broad information exposure may begin to tell a disproportionately expansive story about private lives, so too might it risk telling a muddled or digressive story that drowns useful analytical signals in a sea of irrelevant, potentially misleading noise. A set of methods to limit the disclosure of data in accordance with and responsive to the specific nature of the inquiry at hand is needed.

Data-revelation practices for controlled data exposure must often be formulated and implemented to address privacy, data security, and analytic efficiency concerns that arise in a given context for information usage. Failure to adopt these practices can create or amplify the hazards of data breaches, allow for scope creep (whereby data users may deliberately or inadvertently transgress the bounds of their initial objective by virtue of a lack of exposure constraints), and create mosaic effects from unrestricted comingling of data types.

Requirements of Data Revelation

Data-revelation regimes are intended to promote proportionality in the exposure and use of sensitive, personally identifying data. The overarching idea is to minimize information disclosure in such a way so as to not materially constrain the ability of authorized users to make appropriate use of the data. Ideally, the revealed data should therefore be equivalent in value with the data that would be exposed if such privacy protections were not in place.[2] In other words, minimization should optimize on cutting as much fat as possible, without cutting (too deeply) into the meat. In practice,

---

2 Sweeney, Latanya. "Privacy-Preserving Surveillance using Selective Revelation." Carnegie Mellon University, LIDAP Working Paper 15, 2005.

this can be challenging, though as we will see later, there are ways to address this issue based on empirical analysis.

The intent of exacting exposure of information is not to prevent users from accessing information to which they have rightful authority. Rather, it's to provide a clear, accountable mechanism for ensuring those rightful authorities are adhered to under the appropriate circumstances. As such, as information is being revealed, impediments to access should be minimized as much as possible. An onerous, process-heavy implementation that makes access to sensitive data under appropriate and authorized circumstances unwieldy or worse is perhaps as undesirable an outcome as a framework in which data is indiscriminately disclosed.

Exposure procedures should also ensure the data revealed under particular circumstances is proportionately responsive to the originating justification. Data access parsimony for its own sake is undesirable if it means users must jump through a series of ongoing, unnecessary procedural hoops to gain access to the full set of data required and authorized for their work.

In the following section, we'll discuss some practical principles for setting the appropriate scope of revealed data to help enforce this principle of proportionality, especially as a substitute in circumstances where other governing access or exposure principles do not exist.

Selective Revelation

Selective revelation refers to disclosing or sharing information to a varying degree, proportionate to the needs of the intended use case.[3] By limiting data exposure in proportion to the conditions of the originating query while remaining compliant with relevant laws, guidelines, or other terms, both privacy and analytical objectives are served.

Application of selective revelation in an information system might involve the degree of exposure of a physical address. Addresses are locational identifiers made up of components that together provide levels of geolocational specificity. For instance, the fictional address of 123 Main Street, Apt. 7F, Springfield, IL, USA 62073 is comprised of the component elements in Figure 7-1. The association of a residence, event, or person with this address might constitute an act of sensitive data disclosure. However, the degree of sensitivity can be limited by gradually and proportionally modulating the degree of exposure of the full address.

---

3 The definition offered here is intentionally phrased as a weaker version of Sweeney's more scientifically rigorous formulation in "Privacy-Preserving Surveillance using Selective Revelation."

Number	Street	Apartment	City	State	Country	Zip
971	Tory Lane		Cambridge	Massachusetts	USA	02137
11	Jade Court	43	Albuquerque	New Mexico	USA	87120
123	Main Street	7F	Springfield	Illinois	USA	62073
156	Friedrichstrasse	29	Berlin		Germany	10969
5	Merry Way		Newark	New Jersey	USA	07302
56	W Long Street	8G	Columbus	Ohio	USA	43215

Figure 7-1. Selective Revelation can be applied to certain data elements, such as addresses, that are composed of multiple parts. By excluding or revealing select address elements, a system can provide the necessary degree of data exposure required for the purpose at hand without revealing too much locational information about the underlying data subject.

For example, imagine an analysis aimed at understanding whether urban or rural residents are more likely to own pickup trucks. In this case, even though a vehicle registry system may contain the full addresses of all registered automobiles, the complete address does not need to be exposed to the analyst in order to complete the task. Instead, it would be sufficient to disclose the city, state, and zip code corresponding to each vehicle and its type. With those limited address components, the analyst would be able to check against an established directory of urban and rural locales to determine that, for example, a specific pickup truck registered to "Springfield, IL, 62073" is associated with an urban resident.

However, if the analyst was tasked with determining from the same vehicle registry the Illinois zip code with the highest percentage of multi-vehicle households among all households owning vehicles, it would not be sufficient to merely reveal each registered vehicle's city, state, and zip code. Rather, the analyst would likely need to know the corresponding complete address for each vehicle so that she could then create (again, for each address) a corresponding tally of registered vehicles. Finally, the analyst could then calculate for each zip code the count of all such unique addresses with greater than one registered vehicle divided by the total number of unique registered addresses.

Selective revelation doesn't necessarily need to involve extreme scenarios like the above (i.e., a case in which only the most general address component is revealed and another in which all address components are revealed). Selective revelation also provides a guiding construct for a range of other permutations of information disclosure corresponding to other analytic contexts. Imagine that our analyst is tasked with determining the percentage of families living in multi-tenant dwellings that drive sedans. In this case, though the analyst will need to be exposed to the most granular address component (i.e., the apartment number, which serves as a proxy indicator of multi-tenant dwellings), all other address components, including the least specific or least locationally informative component (i.e., the country), can be excluded from the data provisioned to the analyst.

In each case, our analyst is exposed only to the component(s) needed for each of the analytical tasks. In so doing, each analytical task involves disclosure of location-identifying information that is directly proportional to the requirements of the task at hand. No more and no less.[4]

Purpose-Driven Revelation

Purpose-driven revelation is a variation of data-revelation techniques in which the degree, type, or classification of information exposure is contingent upon and determined by the specification of a predicate or search purpose.

For example, in response to public concern for the potential privacy harms associated with unmitigated exposure of sensitive information previously collected by automatic license plate readers (ALPR), a law enforcement agency might adopt a set of authorized purposes only under which the ALPR data may be queried and analyzed.[5] Those purpose requirements may be enforced in a manner that requires users to certify the respective authorized purpose with each query, along with any additional optional or mandatory supporting details (e.g., case numbers, case notes, etc.), as in Figure 7-2. Failure to provide an authorized search purpose may prevent the system from completing the requested query, or may trigger a warning or other disciplinary action. Additionally, the query itself may be used to trigger some more formal approval process (manual or automated) that requires a further review or certification of the specified predicate parameters prior to returning the requested information.

Just as with selective revelation, the main reason to use purpose-driven revelation is to constrain the exposure of data by establishing threshold conditions that must be met in order to reveal information. The constraining conditions are often defined by some established set of categories that may be codified in rules, statutes, guidelines, or law. In our previous ALPR case, authorized purposes might include, for example, the

---

4 The granularity at which you can manage data is dependent on the granularity of your access control model. See Chapter 6 on Access Controls for more information.

5 For example, the Northern California Regional Intelligence Center enforces a policy (*http://bit.ly/ncric-alpr*) whereby any search against its ALPR database requires the preliminary entry or certification that the query is pursuant to one of a discrete list of authorized search purposes.

location of a stolen or wanted vehicle, or searches enacted to help track down a missing person.

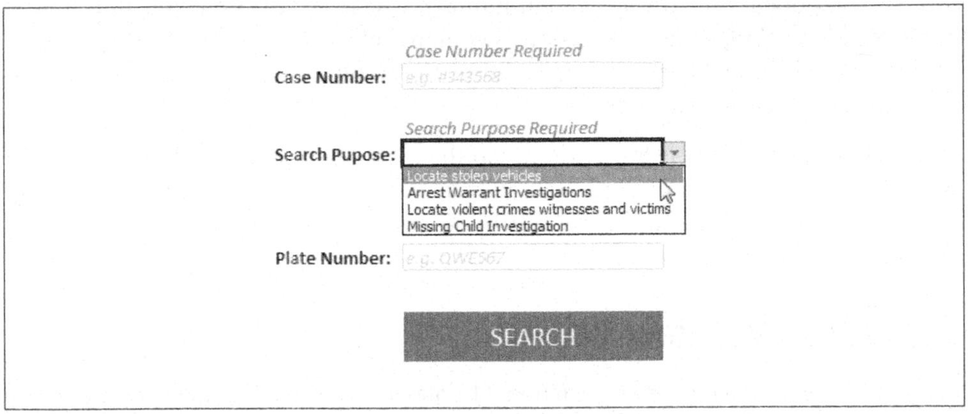

Figure 7-2. The query interface of a system accessing ALPR records may be configured so as to require the entry of a Case Number and Search Purpose as a precondition to returning any related results for the actual license plate number search term.

Scope-Driven Revelation

Scope-driven revelation is another refinement of data-revelation techniques, in which the baseline for determining the extent of data exposure is some type of measure, scale, or boundary condition. A good example of scope-driven revelation occurs in the context of U.S. jurisprudence. In U.S. law enforcement, a search warrant will often be crafted in accordance with some type of reasonableness standard specifying a range of inquiry. For example, a search may be restricted to the contents of a circumscribed physical location or a range of telephone call records.

A few common types of scoping conditions and corresponding examples include:

Temporal scope
> Specifies a time range of records that may be retrieved and exposed by an information system. For example, a database used by a school district for tracking disciplinary activity might be used to enforce a truancy policy, whereby more than three truant days in a given semester results in a suspension. The scope of recall of truancy data returned for any given student for the purpose of this type of disciplinary action would, therefore, be limited to the temporal scope of the current semester.

Spatial scope
> Specifies a locational boundary (e.g., a radius, polygon, or district) within which information can or cannot be revealed. For example, a system used to store and analyze aerial imagery for agricultural research may enforce "geo-fences" around

sensitive areas (e.g., military installations, religious institutions) such that any queries or analyses of the imagery are constrained to exclude or obfuscate details that fall within the sensitive perimeters.

Degrees of separation scope

Specifies a level or levels of relational distance from the initial query parameter or "seed" for which results may be returned by an information system. A now-infamous example of degrees of separation scope-driven revelation is the telephony metadata analysis regime enacted under Section 215 of the USA PATRIOT Act whereby NSA analysts were permitted license to review metadata associated with phone calls as distant as three levels or "hops" removed from the initial seed telephone number.

In order for scope-driven revelation to work, the information source needs a mechanism for efficient retrieval according to the scoping parameters. Typically, this means that metadata associated with the records in question (e.g., timestamps, geo-coordinates, and taxonomic classifications) exist and have been indexed for rapid query and recall. Frequently, those indices may be readily available, as these limiting parameters are regularly used already as standard search criteria. However, the application of search indices for scope-driven revelation differs from a more conventional search, where additional limiting parameters may be applied. In the scope-driven case, the limitations are compulsory and predetermined by some other rule- or predicate-oriented parameter, whereas in the standard search case, the conditions are optional and must be explicitly specified as query filters.

Hybrid Revelation and Practical Scoping

In many practical settings, the data-revelation techniques outlined above are best employed jointly. Consider our earlier ALPR example. It may be that specific search purposes statutorily dictate distinct temporal scopes of revealed license plate reads. That is, while search queries citing "Parking Violation" as the search purpose may only entitle the law enforcement analyst to a view of a rolling window of ten days of ALPR reads, queries enacted in support of "Missing Child" cases may justify the revelation of query results dating back two years. In this case, the severity of the search purpose determines the specific time frame of allowable result, providing a flexible framework for hybrid data revelation that accommodates a range of investigative use cases.

Similar to purpose-driven revelation, the scoping conditions may be a function of established legal or policy principles. However, because scope-driven revelation often entails quantifiable measures, it is also possible to determine scoping conditions by empirical, data-driven analysis.

Again, drawing on our ALPR example, there might not exist *a priori* sound reasons for restricting the temporal or spatial ranges of ALPR query results subject to any particular search predicate. Analysis of previous investigation outcomes, however, may provide sufficient, reliable signal to empirically assert appropriate scoping conditions. For example, if 95% of stolen vehicle cases that have been solved using ALPR technology involve vehicle recovery within a ten-mile radius of the reported site of the theft, this fact could serve as a credible determinant for codifying the appropriate spatial range of ALPR results respondent to "stolen vehicle" search predicates. In this example, analysis might indicate that while expanding search results to a 100-mile radius might solve an additional 2% of stolen vehicle cases, that marginal improvement does not weigh favorably or proportionally against the potentially resultant harm to the privacy of the additional drivers who might have their vehicle movements unjustifiably scrutinized as part of the additional data reach.

Designing for Data Revelation

The data-revelation methodologies explained in this chapter can often be readily implemented against most backend infrastructures (e.g., SQL and noSQL databases) that are already designed to support efficient recall of data. This often implies that the most pressing design concerns relate to the user interfaces through which data is requested and retrieved. In practice, this may translate into some tight accommodation of entry fields. Search interfaces may need to be restrictive in focusing query predicates on the terms or parameters that best express only the range of acceptable results and nothing more, as opposed to enabling universally flexible, open-ended query parameters that are much more prone to over-exposing data. Mandatory entry fields (e.g., fields requiring the entry of correctly parsed or otherwise validated search predicates or case numbers) may also need to be built into the user interface to ensure query conditions are adequately and appropriately specified.

One of the most significant challenges in determining entry parameters is establishing the appropriate search predicates and the corresponding range, type, or form of acceptable result sets. Accordingly, an effort to define upfront a clear set of policies to be instantiated in the design will go a long way in directing technical decisions. Where policies or other guidelines may not have clear precedent, empirical analysis of existing data may provide a sound starting point for establishing practical, data-driven conditions for the scope of revealed information.

Strengths and Weaknesses of Data Revelation

Like access controls, there are many potential configurations and permutations of data-revelation methods that may be employed to address systems' requirements, policies, or implementation guidelines. Deciding on whether the application of these techniques justifies the engineering cost and user impact requires weighing the applicable strengths and weaknesses in the context of each proposed application.

Strengths

The primary strengths to consider in evaluating whether to implement data revelation methods are as follows:

Precision
> Data-revelation techniques provide mechanisms for fine-tuned, limited exposure of data. The degree of precision can be honed to arbitrary precision, depending on the granularity to which predicate conditions can be specified and applied to query results.

Nuance
> The level of specificity implied by selective, purpose-, and scope-driven revelation-exposure methods enables nuanced information retrieval that goes far beyond the more common circumstance of undefined or ill-defined justifications for drawing upon an available data store. The more nuance that can be introduced in both querying and returning information, the more responsive the results may be to the specific analytical context, and the smaller the risk of overexposed data.

Accountability
> By serving as required predicates that must be entered as preconditions for search queries, these techniques (especially purpose-driven revelation) introduce additional, context-specific curation of user interactions with the information system. By logging these predicates against the search event, the conditions can later be viewed as reference points to ensure authorized or appropriate use of the system. Moreover, by forcing users to *actively* assert their justifications for seeking certain data elements, these methods impose additional psychological impediments to malfeasance.[6]

Weaknesses

Conversely, data revelation methods may not always make sense for a given application, and it's worth considering the following weaknesses to make a well-informed architectural decision:

---

6 A user may think twice about searching for ALPR reads related to an ex's vehicle if the user must first assert a search purpose that plainly does not authorize such a query.

Pre-planning required
> Though these tools are powerful for restricting exposure when well-defined query parameters exist and are codified in policy or law, without such conditions, applying these techniques can be much more complicated. The limitation has less to do with technical restrictions and more to do with an organization's ability to establish and codify rule sets. For example, organizations may struggle with determining whether two or three degrees of relational linking constitutes a justifiable or overreaching query. Without the political will either to set an appropriately restrictive predicate or to carry out the necessary (and potentially costly) empirical study to determine sensible standards, organizations may opt for no scope specification at all.

Resistance to highly complex conditions
> Environments with massive rule sets that are hard to codify or difficult to administer may introduce such significant complexity and onerousness in the implementation of data-revelation techniques as to make their usage impractical.

Lack of flexibility
> While these features and techniques are well-suited to environments with established and commonly occurring rule sets, they may be less desirable or useable in other settings. Frequently changing or exigent circumstances might substantially alter and unpredictably dictate the appropriate uses of information and prove an impediment to data-revelation techniques. Analytical regimes that consist primarily of exploratory analysis involving dynamic permutations of data in nonminimized forms may not accommodate these methods of restricted data exposure.

Data Revelation and the Fair Information Practice Principles (FIPPs)

The implementation of data-revelation techniques is essential in upholding the following FIPPs:

Purpose specification
> These techniques inculcate a data exposure regime in which information may only be revealed in accordance with established and codified purposes that typically must be asserted and documented as a precondition to accessing the requested data.

Use limitation
> By enforcing gradated, conditionally restrictive retrieval of information, these techniques can further refine the exposure and use of data to help mitigate the risks of information becoming casually repurposed for applications that extend beyond the initial collection or retrieval justifications.

Collectively, we might think of these FIPPs as constituting a notion of proportional data exposure. Data used in a given scenario should comport with some set of well-defined, deliberate, and purposeful justifications that sufficiently limit the extent of revealed data. In turn, such deliberate and disciplined exposure assists the user in accomplishing authorized tasks without creating unnecessary risks of over-exposure of information.

When to Use Data Revelation

Selective, purpose-, and scope-driven revelation techniques tend to be most effective when clear rules for their application can be defined at the outset or through preliminary analysis. These techniques tend to find fertile ground in information regimes governed by existing terms, laws, or other guidelines that apply binding constraints on the ability of the data to support authorized tasks or activities. Terms of service or posted privacy policies might, for example, outline clear conditions for both the purposing and scoping of end users' personally identifying information.

Conclusion

Selective, purpose-, and scope-driven data-revelation techniques provide a powerful set of privacy enhancing tools by contextually refining data exposure and enforcing practical circumstances of need-to-know. Used in conjunction with a robust application of access controls to ensure right-to-know principles, these techniques can round out a data system's framework for exposing information to end users, thereby mitigating risks of privacy harms through unauthorized and unjustifiable information retrieval and usage.

PART III

Oversight: Holding Users and Systems Accountable

The second of our broad capability umbrellas is oversight. Oversight refers to mechanisms that allow appropriately authorized system users to monitor how data is used in order to ensure compliance with whatever legal, ethical, and other imperatives govern data usage. In Chapter 8, we look at how federated systems can enable data sharing while allowing the data controller to maintain oversight of the data. Chapter 9 explores the potential of audit logs to provide detailed insight into data usage as a means of enforcing rigorous privacy policy. In Chapter 10, we discuss the ultimate oversight decision by which data is removed from a system entirely and effectively returned to the sole control of the data subject once again.

CHAPTER 8

Federated Systems

Overview

People often want to run queries across multiple sources of data because the information they're looking for is spread out over many different places. However, searching individually through each data source quickly becomes cumbersome and tedious. It's also costly to build a search interface for each and every data source. On the other hand, putting all of your possibly-relevant data in a single data warehouse can be wasteful and unsecure. It requires lots of duplicative data (frequently riddled with copying errors) and presents attackers with a single target that, once breached, will compromise all your sensitive data.

Federated data systems make it possible to search for, find, retrieve, and view data from multiple sources (both internal or external) by using a single coherent interface, and do not require all of that data to be stored in a single monolithic database. Data is left in place at its source, secured and managed by each source system's owners, and end users can view and interact with all of the data relevant to their activities. In some cases, users might be conscious of the fact that their data is stored in separate systems. In other cases, the system may behave as if all the pieces of data were all in a single database dedicated to the application they use. Either way, federated systems offer a convenient user experience without compromising the security of the data within it, and different kinds of federated architectures offer different technical and policy advantages with regard to privacy.

This can be a tremendous advantage. It's not always possible for your system to directly hold all relevant data. At times, a third-party web service might not give you a copy of all the data it holds, but will agree to let you search its holdings selectively. Alternately, the data might be held in an Internet-accessible web service that, instead of giving you direct access to the data, only exposes a web-based query API.

You may not want to store it all anyway. With federation, you can keep the relevant data in different databases in order to scale beyond what can fit in a single one. A federated setup works well when source systems might need to keep archives of historical data, but your use case might only need the most recent data. Setting up a dedicated federated search service also brings maintenance benefits; you can take just one server offline at a time without requiring a full system outage.

Given the privacy risks of monolithic databases, it's not always desirable to hold all the data in one place. Monolithic databases attract unwanted attention given the vast troves of information inside. They can also be unwieldy for security purposes—it's hard to keep track of traffic, and it's increasingly difficult to scale encryption methods. If that one database is cracked, all of its information is compromised. Additionally, a single database may not reliably separate confidential information from more generic data, opening the way for future abuse that could be avoided by federation.

"Always-On" Federation

Federated search manages to keep data separate by maintaining an index of the structured and unstructured external data sources without copying them in their entirety into a central data store. By scanning the source systems at regular intervals, the federated search service ensures the index is kept up-to-date. When a search returns matches, they can be imported to an enterprise-level data repository in a server to which users' clients connect. Simultaneously, links between each piece of returned data and its corresponding record in the original source system are preserved, thus reflecting any deletions or updates to the original data performed by the data owners. Users who work with this data never need to check whether they have the latest version; the federated system is keeping it up-to-date for them in the background.

Federated search offers design advantages on both ends of the workflow. For administrators, this design makes it possible for data owners to maintain responsibility and control over their information. This includes setting variable and appropriate access controls (where necessary) to prevent unauthorized use. For users, searching and viewing results with an always-on federated system feels indistinguishable from using a single centralized data store, even though the servers and database architectures may be different. Once the users authenticate and log on to an authorized system interface, they have access to all stored and federated data through the same interface. This cohesive experience respects all underlying security permissions, keeps the data up to date, and sidesteps any need for the user to manually and laboriously check through different databases separately.

Asynchronous Federation

Another form of federated system involves a far more loosely interconnected set of databases. In this configuration, the various distributed database components are not always connected and running an index in the background, but instead communicate sporadically with each other at the user's request to share and update information. When not connected, the databases function completely separately.

When setting up a federated system that isn't constantly tracking all data modifications on all ends, it becomes important to keep a versioned history of changes to the same data. For example, imagine a health analyst has been working on a project in which she finds data about a disease outbreak in Database A. She copies it to a separate system in which she'll do her work. She'll only need to connect to Database A every few weeks because other researchers, who are using it too, only update the database with their findings once or twice a month.

Meanwhile, our analyst digs into the outbreak, which happened at Restaurant 1. She concludes that Restaurant 1's disease outbreak is quite similar to another outbreak at Restaurant 2, suggesting there might be a causal factor her team can trace back to a shared supplier. She adds a link between Restaurants 1 and 2, and continues her work. Unbeknownst to her, while she was doing this, another researcher across the country was also working on the outbreak at Restaurant 1, and concluded that Restaurant 3 may be involved as well. He goes ahead and links it to Restaurant 1.

There are now three versions of the outbreak record for Restaurant 1: the original in the source system, the one our first analyst is working with that she's linked to Restaurant 2, and the one the other researcher has separately linked to Restaurant 3.

When our first analyst uploads her findings to Database A, her remote colleague will not know about it until he next connects to Database A. Unlike the "always-on" federation model, his data will not automatically update or prompt him right away with a notice that new information is available. However, once either analyst connects after the other's modified data becomes available, the federated architecture will need to have a component that tracks the version history of the data with all the different modifications.

This notional example, illustrated in Figure 8-1, involves only three pieces of data and two users, but the complexity increases rapidly with scale. If our first analyst made modifications to the Restaurant 3 record while doing her analysis, or if her colleague enriched Restaurant 1's record with new information, and her analysis depends upon this change, the system will not only need to track data history and versions, but it will also be able to propose deconfliction pathways when data sharing is asynchronous.

The astute reader may notice that this sounds very similar to distributed version control for source code, as embodied in systems such as Git or Mercurial. Make no mistake: building this sort of distributed system is fraught with challenges.[1] However, there is substantial research regarding various techniques that are useful when implementing the necessary accounting. A few of these logical clocking algorithms for distributed data systems are vector and matrix clocks, Lamport timestamps, plausible clocks, and interval tree clocks. The complexity of your system will guide the selection of a causal reasoning method that's appropriate for your use cases.

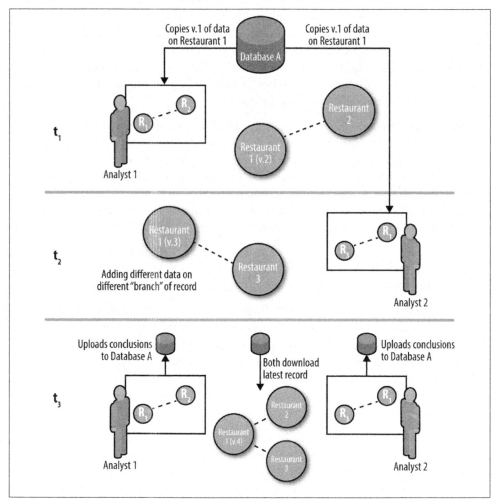

Figure 8-1. Versioned data merged and deconflicted via asynchronous federation.

---

1 For a description of such a system in practice, see Nexus Peering: Solving the Inter-Organizational Data Sharing Problem (*http://bit.ly/palantir-nexus*).

Asking Out and Being Asked

There are a few different forms a federated system can take. The two versions of which we have described above federate out to multiple other systems, and are primarily used for searching the contents of other systems. But another kind of system functions more as a federated *source*; it is searched by one or more external systems and it requires decisions to be made about what to make available to outside queries. We might call this a shared federated search server, and it offers different benefits. We've represented these two types of systems in Figure 8-2. A federated data source, P, has made two subsets of its total data holdings available for searching to the federation. System Y federates out to (queries and draws from) multiple external systems (P, Q, R, and S), each of which is making available its own subsets of data—represented by the shaded sectors—to this querying system.

The first decisions when setting up such a shared federated source have to do with the *what*, aka the data. After determining what data to share overall, you must decide what fraction of that shared data should be shared with each external system that will search it, whether it will always be the same information, or whether one external system only will have access to one subset of the shared data while a different external system will have access to a different subset.

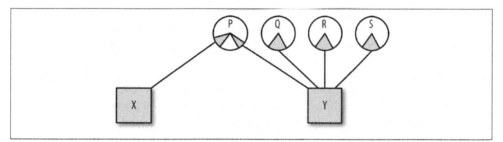

Figure 8-2. A notional data federation drawing from four external federated data sources.

The next decisions involve *who*, aka your users. You may need to assign variable permissions to the different sets of users of the external systems that are searching the shared federated data. This could require an access control regime that mirrors the access control regimes of those systems, or a role-based regime if there's foreknowledge of who will be searching, along with a way to verify the searcher's role.

Finally, there is the question of *how*: whether the data will be shared as full, individual records, as partial views of records, as just the metadata, or as aggregate statistics on the data. The latter options are particularly useful from a privacy perspective because, as noted in Chapter 3, it's often unnecessary to share the specifics of the underlying data. This can reduce or eliminate incentives to release sensitive information.

Strengths and Weaknesses of Federated Systems

Federated architecture is not one-size-fits-all. One criticism sometimes leveled at federated systems is that comprehensive analysis is only possible when the relevant data is all held in the same centralized repository. However, existing technologies developed over the past decade have proven that this criticism no longer applies, and can even be addressed at scale.

Strengths

The following are a few strengths of federated systems pertaining to implementation:

Scalability and flexibility
> It's often not possible to store all relevant data in your main system's dedicated database. With a federated architecture, it's possible to take advantage of both increased data access (more users) and horizontal data scaling (more data with less hardware overhead). Total aggregation is also often unnecessary and needlessly expensive. Federated solutions can deal with large sets of information while costing less, since there's no need to build a new, central database when the smaller pre-existing databases can now be shared.

Unified UX
> Data can be left in place, presenting a single cohesive view of all relevant distributed data to authorized users without requiring another copy of the data.

Ease of maintenance
> Using a dedicated server or set of servers whose sole purpose is federated search improves search capabilities across the whole system. Data owners can use a federated data architecture to maintain responsibility for and control over their data's use and accuracy even after sharing it with other authorized parties.

Redundancy
> If a data source goes offline, your users—especially those who only need information from the other data sources that are still online—can still make use of your system.

Precise control
> In addition to enabling broader searches when appropriate, by allowing (or requiring) users to specify which data sources to query, a federated architecture can help enforce policies such as search justifications (see Chapter 7) and provide for more detailed logs for audit records. Federation also preserves the data-handling rules and policies implemented in each pre-existing database. Often, these rules exist and differ from each other for good reasons. This logic often becomes blurred when moving disparate data to a single central database, caus-

ing confusion regarding the appropriate data-handling rules that should apply to a particular piece of data.

Simplified per-system security
It's easier to make smaller, separate databases secure than one large, especially tempting target. By including expiring caches of the search results, the federated search service doesn't need to store returned data for longer than the user's session (resolution of duplicate data can also be temporary). Federated architecture reduces the amount of data at risk of compromise. It's much easier for an attacker to break into a single database where all the relevant information is stored than to breach multiple, discrete, repositories.

Weaknesses

Some weaknesses to consider in evaluating whether to implement federated solutions are as follows:

Performance
Federated search requires extra steps that may cause slower searches than querying an internal database directly. Connecting to an external system, translating a search in your system to a data-source-specific query, passing the translated query to that data source, and returning data from the relevant external systems all take extra work and time. In addition, data access and uptime issues may arise due to any network reliability issues from external source systems.

Coding discipline issues
It can be tempting to write a federated search program the first time you encounter an external data source, but it will likely be overly specific to that system. In order to make future development easier, especially for additional unanticipated data-sources, it's worth considering implementing a generic federated search service and specific data source API. It's also difficult to coordinate and collaborate among multiple database administrators. A federated data system sometimes involves different legal and ethical imperatives, or even just different, strongly held opinions on procedure. Designing a federated system will require you to come to some agreement as to how to administer the system (Democratic agreement? Contract? Dictatorial fiat?) and then to have some mechanism to hold others in the system accountable for deviations from the agreement.

Larger overall attack surface
A federated search service can act as a user on each of the connected data sources, and if compromised, could provide an attacker with access to them. While a federated data system avoids the disadvantages of a single central data store, it also expands the system's trust boundary to multiple organizations and external users and can still present a large attack surface. A successful attacker's access

would be limited by the source system's access-control regime, assuming the compromised account lacked the ability to escalate access privileges. But if users access the federation through an interface (such as MySQL over TLS or VPN) that allows privilege escalations, an attacker could use that to access much more than system administrators intended for any given user account. Another risk is that one site may cache the data it acquires through data federation, at which point a compromise of that site would mean a compromise of not just that site's data but a portion of the federation's data as well. These risks should be considered in any system design and implementation.

Loss of wholesale control
If multiple users and administrators have access to the data, users cannot always fully rely on data integrity. Policies and procedures for maintaining data accuracy and integrity will vary from database to database, potentially compromising the value of the entire data corpus due to inconsistencies in data quality.

Federated Systems and the Fair Information Practice Principles (FIPPs)

As with access controls and data-revelation techniques, federated architecture is instrumental in upholding various FIPPs in the following ways:

Collection limitation
By leaving data in separate repositories and not combining it with other data in novel, unanticipated ways, a federated architecture helps ensure information is used only for the purposes for which it was originally collected.

Data quality
By reflecting updates and corrections made in original source systems, a federated architecture helps ensure search results return accurate data, avoiding errors and misidentifications that can lead to privacy violations.

Purpose specification and use limitation
By maintaining data in separate source systems and preserving data owners' control, a federated system may be configured to require anyone requesting data to explain why they need it and receive authorization before gaining access.

Security
By avoiding aggregating data into a single database, a federated architecture reduces the chance of total data exposure in the event of unauthorized access.

Openness and individual participation
By maintaining smaller databases that feed into a larger system, redress requirements can be spread among multiple database administrators. This allows more personalized service, reduces the overall burden of database administration, and

that ensures updates to information requested by individual data subjects in the system are propagated system-wide. Another option is to create a central hub connected to multiple databases, which could also allow for a centralization of redress where an individual only has to go to a single database administrator to correct information in multiple systems. In short, there are multiple models available to help users access and correct information about themselves.

When to Use Federated Architecture

Federated architecture is more suitable in some circumstances than in others. In some cases, technical or policy considerations will dictate a more centralized solution or some combination of centralization of some data sources and federation of others. But given certain factors, a federated solution is likely best.

Complex Regulatory Regimes

Though many countries share some baseline similarities regarding privacy (e.g., FIPPs), they can vary greatly in detail. Given the ease and frequency with which data crosses international borders, many data systems are quickly going to find themselves housing data with any number of country-specific handling requirements. One option might simply be to apply the most restrictive data protection to all of the data in the system (the "highest common denominator," perhaps). But data-protection requirements cannot be so easily arranged into a strict hierarchy of weak to strong. In some cases, regimes even directly contradict each other. Blanket restrictions may also needlessly undermine the overall utility of your product. A more granular implementation of the individually applicable laws might result in a more effective product while still offering the desired level of privacy protection.

Federated systems facilitate such data handling. By sorting information into databases according to categories dictated by law, such as geography, data type, or others, a federated system can create clear boundaries between data sets. Policy and technical controls can be applied based on the physical location of the data. As long as the data is persistently sourced to those servers, users, administrators, then oversight authorities can quickly identify the applicable handling requirements. In addition, in the event that a particular data set is found to be out of compliance with legal requirements, the particular data set can be taken offline (either permanently or temporarily for remediation) while allowing the rest of the system to continue to operate. The fact that a data set can be taken offline individually is helpful when adjusting to ever-changing policies.

Lack of Trust

Federated architecture obviates the need for the data provider to assume all risk based on trust in the recipient of the data. A significant barrier to free information exchange is a lack of trust in other participants in the data-sharing network. Once data slips from the direct control of a data provider, the provider must rely on the recipient of the data to handle the information responsibly. In many cases, particularly where the data provider may be exposed to significant legal liability or customer outrage should the data be misused, this uncertainty prevents information sharing that would otherwise benefit both parties. As data scale increases, so does potential liability for breach or misuse. The willingness to rely simply on contract provisions and trust as protection against potentially crippling damages awards wanes accordingly.

In a federated system, the data provider maintains a server of data that is entirely under their control yet still accessible to the data recipient. The data provider can monitor all search queries and access events, and, if necessary, even approve or deny access requests in order to tightly control the data flow from their servers. Even when data leaves the provider's server, it can remain tethered to its original sources, allowing the data provider to correct or update inaccurate or out-of-date information and push those updates to data recipients.

In addition, a federated system can be configured to allow the data provider to retroactively revoke access to data that has already been shared, removing it from the recipient's view within a matter or moments. For this configuration to work, the client software has to be implemented such that it automatically updates itself (periodically or immediately) to reflect changes in the data on the server. Such a design also assumes a certain level of trust of users that they won't modify the client software, take screenshots, or conduct memory forensics to recover the data removed from their view. There is no perfect guarantee that the client software has fully performed a server instruction to erase or stop displaying data, but we believe the data provider can maintain a high level of control that ultimately encourages a greater amount of data sharing throughout the network.

PR Imperatives

"Big databases are creepy."

While this is not a particularly helpful articulation of the concern, it is one that system architects are likely to encounter as they construct ever-larger, centralized repositories of data. While effective use limitations (both through access controls and oversight) might address the actual practical concerns that people have about data use, the image of the single gargantuan database remains troubling to many people concerned about privacy.

Federated architecture provides the functionality of a single database while avoiding the negative perceptions associated with centralization. This is more than just window dressing. While the federated system still provides centralized access to data, the centralization only occurs when specifically needed in support of a particular use case rather than dumping all the data together at the outset when it may not necessarily ever be needed by the centralized system.

Conclusion

Federated system architecture offers numerous advantages. The specifics of any given implementation will vary, depending on factors such as the number of data sources, their size and respective security regimes, expected number of concurrent users, and data-retention laws and policies. Combining federation with the other access methods discussed can contribute to the larger goal of responsible data stewardship and oversight.

CHAPTER 9

Audit Logging

Overview

Audit records are a critical but often poorly understood and executed feature of information systems. Effective auditing for a substantive oversight regime requires a great measure of thoughtfulness and planning at the outset, and various considerations must be addressed in engineering and architectural decisions to help provide a sound audit framework. When properly designed and implemented, audit records can help systems administrators, data stewards, and institutions more confidently provide for accountability, trust, and reduced risk and liability.

Why Are Audit Records Important?

Earlier, we noted that application-level security involves two key aspects: access control and oversight. We then discussed how restrictions imposed through access controls and data-revelation techniques enforce necessary requirements for a privacy-friendly system but are not sufficient by themselves. This is because as long as there are access controls that allow access to any sensitive data, there are ways in which that access can be abused. Beyond access controls and selective data-exposure techniques, organizations need infrastructure for effective oversight, which will allow for the *careful observations of the use of the system*. Only through active monitoring and oversight of the system can the risks posed by legitimate access be managed and mitigated.

Auditability is critical not just for internal verification purposes but also for asserting accountability to regulatory authorities. It also helps address questions of public or data subject trust, and can ensure data access is not being abused, either through willful malfeasance or (more often) negligence. The ability to point to effective, reliable audit trails can serve as a key element of defending an enterprise against charges of malfeasance, assist in rapidly investigating suspected data breaches, and demonstrate compliance with legal and policy obligations.

But Auditing Is Easy, Right?

It's commonly assumed that auditing is a straightforward, basic task. Many information systems already tout some form of auditing or audit logging, often to satisfy a line item in the original system requirement around auditability. Unfortunately, the common-but-simplistic requirement of *must create an auditable log* does not typically translate to the production of *usable* audit logs or ensure the institution of *effective* auditing practices.

Frequently, the audit trails that already exist within information systems are relics from earlier system development and function more as tools for providing debugging information than for accountability or oversight. They persist in this form because auditing capabilities are generally regarded as perfunctory—boxes to check off on a systems requirements list, with no bearing on the core functionality or effectiveness of the system. Even audit-logging capabilities that are engineered for oversight functions often fail to take into consideration the nuances of operational oversight workflows, and ultimately prove inadequate when it becomes necessary to employ those logs for practical auditing applications.

Truly usable and effective auditing capabilities require nontrivial technical and strategic considerations. The system needs to be designed to address the constraints and requirements of complex enterprises spanning many user types, data systems, and auditing foci. Even seemingly low-level auditing of information systems entails complexities that are often poorly understood, leading to suboptimal implementations that can ultimately impede or outright undermine organizational ability to conduct meaningful audit analysis.

What Are the Challenges to Effective Auditing and How Do I Meet Them?

The challenges to engineering and implementing an effective auditing regime are manifold and complex. However, there are a few key difficulties and corresponding minimum requirements that can be anticipated and should be addressed by systems architects when considering a rounded approach to creating audit infrastructure. Some of these considerations exist in tension with each other. As with all design exercises, there are no canonical answers here but only a balancing of the right set of tradeoffs that meets the needs of the context and system at hand.

Perspective

In order to support effective audit analytics, audit records must be able to support a range of perspectives with which to view and analyze the use of sensitive information. If audit logs are overly rigid in the views they expose, the captured data may be incapable of supporting the types of auditing that prove most essential to ensuring the proper use of an information system. For example, logs that have been created to support the debugging of system errors on a system's backend may entail an overly detailed record of server-side manipulations but be insufficient to reconstruct the manner in which data is used by the frontend user. This would severely limit the ability of auditors to investigate potential user malfeasance. A simple example might be a log that records each discrete step the backend takes in loading records from the data store but fails to record the original query that generated the loading action in the first place.

In order to provide the flexibility needed to support the necessary audit record interactions and assessment angles demanded by the relevant auditing requirements, auditors must consider the actual questions they anticipate asking—i.e., what are the types of stories about user behavior that may need to be reconstructed from the logs. Each anticipated story must be further disected to help determine which facet of the system provides the appropriate view into user actions that will ensure the necessary data is captured.

It's useful to break down these orthogonal perspectives on the actions taking place inside the system into a matrix (Table 9-1). The rows divide the potentially recorded actions into those associated with client-side and server-side interactions. The columns then separate the data values into various characterizations of how an auditor might prefer to interact with the assorted possible representations of the audit metadata—all of them generated for the same user action.

Table 9-1. Determining the right perspective to offer in your audit log output should factor in preferences for the facet of your system (i.e., client- or server-side) arrayed against the type of data representations (i.e., user-, database-, or entity-centric) that are most useful for your system oversight purposes.

	User-centric	Database-centric	Entity-centric
Application/ Client-side	"John Doe" search	User query	Person object displayed in dossier
Server-side	Search application queries for "John" or "Doe"	Table X, column Y, row Z, index value 137	Composition of properties a, b, c loaded for transmission to client

Settling on the desired configuration of the above parameters is an important prerequisite to establishing an audit framework because the decision may have profound implications for the level and location of logging that should be specified. The amount of storage capacity required to support more verbose perspectives; the types of storage, compression, and encryption methods to adopt; and the tools required to subsequently parse and process logs in order to support efficient retrieval can all affect the success of an auditing program. Audit administrators who fail to ask the right questions upfront and appropriately address their implications may later find themselves in the unfortunate position of having approached audit logs collection from an inadequate or inappropriate perspective. At that point, it is often too late to retroactively correct the mistake, leaving behind a trail of mostly useless audit records.

Context

Mastering the right perspective for representing audit records alone will not be adequate to provide auditors with a clear understanding of how users may have interacted with sensitive records in accordance with or in breach of policy. Without additional information to help contextualize the basic content of audit logs, auditors may struggle to make sense of audit trails and may be prone to drawing false or misleading conclusions. Placed in context, seemingly innocuous behavior may prove negligent or worse, while actions that seem nefarious on the surface may have perfectly sensible explanations. Contextual clues may be signaled by various considerations. For example:

- Consistency with historical activity associated with the specific user
- Consistency with activity associated with users of a similar role
- Sequence of activity
- Full scope of information accessed in a given user session

But a basic audit record is often little more than an isolated element. It's potentially just a line of information representing little more than the raw format of data as generated by the system's auditing utilities. If you're lucky, it might have some parsing to make the content more readable (e.g., see Figure 9-1).

```
User SK254 Accessed Datasource 342
```

Figure 9-1. A relatively simple view of audit records that have been formatted for human readability might provide a tabular construction to enable viewing, sorting, and some basic level of analysis.

The inclusion of additional related actions can, however, fill out the full context needed to understand the appropriateness of a user's actions. By composing a comprehensive view of these related actions, an auditor is given a much clearer picture wich which to judge user behavior, including other contextually relevant data ponts and, even more ideally, visualizations to better frame and analyze the audit records. (e.g., see Figure 9-2).

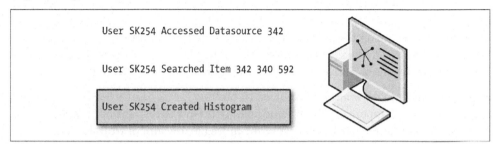

Figure 9-2. A more sophisticated view of audit records might further contextualize individual records by listing related user actions along with additional tools for visually inspecting those records to help the analyst uncover relationships or patterns that may better indicate authorized use or misuse.

One practical consideration of recording context has to do with the timeliness of when the data is logged. Make sure to capture all ephemeral data needed to fully reconstruct and display the context of an audit record before that data becomes entirely irretrievable. For example, an IP address of a client hitting a web service is an easy thing to capture on a web server. But on a dynamically configured network, tying that IP address to an individual user may require traversing two additional data stores: the DHCP server which assigns an IP address to a MAC address on the network and the inventory system that ties the MAC address of an Ethernet interface to the person who is the assigned owner of that device containing the interface. If the logs of the DHCP server are not preserved or if the inventory system does not record historical ownership of a device to an individual, recording the IP address alone loses all value and it will be impossible to later determine the identity of the user who made the request using only the IP address. In contrast, if the logging system can resolve an IP address to an individual at the time the web service is accessed, it would be wise to do so. It's important to capture that fact at the time of record creation rather than assuming it can be *lazy loaded* later.

As you consider building out effective auditing capabilities, it's important to consider how much contextual information is needed to make user interactions legible to the auditor. This means thinking about what those contextual signals entail and how much of that information needs to be captured at the time of record creation. Getting this right reduces the amount of time and energy required to do a proper audit of user actions and should help raise the fidelity of those evaluations.

Format and Readability

If the initial critical tasks of designing an audit-logging system are to identify and contextualize the user behaviors that need to tracked, monitored, and understood, then the next task is to unify these into a readable format. This is difficult, because there is no universally adopted standard for audit-log information. Audit-log formats are as diverse and varied as the systems they track. Even in places where there are standard logging formats, like web server request logs (which have questionable value as audit logs—more on this later), there are still a plethora of different standards from which to choose. The lack of consistency in audit formats is, in part, a reflection of the common default objective that motivates log creation and collection.

Generally, audit logs *should* be produced to provide a record of what happened to a system, when it happened, why it happened, and who is responsible for the action. But most logs exist primarily to assist in the more narrow aim of troubleshooting system errors. This motivates developers to generate logs that will aid in resolving a well-defined and anticipated set of system failures rather than those that will enable oversight of system use. Consequently, when attempts are made to adapt or repurpose those same logs for oversight and auditing applications, both the formats and the data they capture often prove to have either too limited or too broad configurability to satisfy the new requirements.

The focus on fixed, nonconfigurable formats designed for discrete troubleshooting or other purposes often results in logging formats that are dense, rigid, and allow only limited parsing or manipulation for more general analytical or forensic objectives. Much of what is recorded relates to the internal state of the system and its components. It's designed to be consulted in the case of easily identifiable exceptions and errors rather than for everyday monitoring of human behavior in using the system. Logs that are designed with these objectives in mind may be resistant to efficient machine processing, let alone nonexpert human readability, without some significant effort to transform them into more amenable formats. These problems of translation become even more pronounced when institutional vulnerabilities must be understood from the broader context of the mosaic of information spanning multiple systems and cannot be inferred solely from the sparse detail relayed by a single log.

Effective auditing must, therefore, be able to bridge the disparate audit trails from all of the contributing systems to create a comprehensive view of cross-system data vulnerabilities and tie them into a concrete record of the user behavior it aims to monitor. In practical terms, this suggests the need for a method or set of methods for processing and translating disparate audit record types into a common, consistent format that is readily convertible into machine- (or even human-) readable formats where user actions (as opposed to system internals) are the first-class events being recorded. This composite provides the framework to begin conducting regular oversight.

Scale

Audit logs are essentially data about data (or metadata) and can even include historical snapshots of the data itself. This collection of data can be massive in volume, with the potential of growing to volumes even greater than the size of the underlying data to which the audit records relate. For example, an audit log associated with the viewing of a sensitive medical record may consist of the following components:

- Username
- Date and time of the viewing
- User interactions with the data (e.g., viewing, modification, printing, etc.)
- A point-in-time snapshot of the medical record (in order to detail what a given system user might have seen) or any modifications, deletions, or additions made to the canonical record

Given that each audit-log entry might contain a copy of the data itself, it's easy to see where the scale of audit logs can become a significant multiple of the original data itself. Additionally, such audit trails need not (and should not) be constrained to manual interactions with the sensitive records. Any programmatic interactions such as data source "ingestion" events, periodic automatic updates, scheduled deletions, and so on should also all be tracked in a similar manner (though in such cases the associated "username" might instead be the automated user or service carrying out the action).

Scaled to the size of a fully operating system, the audit trails generated by these types of interactions can rapidly expand to enormous, even unwieldy sizes. As audit logs grow, the increasing information scale introduces a new set of associated challenges. Records must then be safely stored and made accessible for efficient recall in the event that an audit analysis is necessary, introducing implications to hardware, storage capacity, memory, performance, and security of the audit logs.

Often for security, storage space, or other optimization reasons, the retention of audit records may be relegated to a dedicated auditing system, maintained and resourced with a lower priority than the main system (since auditing is often an afterthought in system design). To further support long-term scaling challenges, the data is often stored in a compressed format to make efficient use of hardware. To secure the sensitive audit data, the logs may also be encrypted to prevent unwanted dissemination. While file compression may enable greater storage capacity, compression makes already hard-to-read and hard-to-process records even more inscrutable. This introduces greater latency and decompression impediments to searching, filtering, and returning the audit records to more readable and usable formats. Furthermore, encryption methods introduce yet another source of latency and administrative overhead when it comes to converting the compressed and encrypted audit records to a more serviceable format, which makes it more difficult to manage the key material needed to perform decompression without compromising the security of the data.

The cumulative effects of latency and other technical hurdles associated with the measures above result in audit logs that are effectively offline archives that require considerable effort and time for conversion to query and use in any meaningful way. As a result, audit logs tend to lie fallow, or, in more alarming scenarios, are mostly forgotten until a situation arises that motivates audit review. When that happens, it's often a crisis situation when timeliness is a primary consideration, at which point auditors discover that they actually cannot effectively make use of the audit logs and are therefore unable to perform expedient audit analytics.

A number of key design parameters follow from the cluster of issues associated with audit-log scale:

- Very detailed audit records are likely to amass more rapidly than less verbose records. It's worth giving some thought to how long you can support the projected velocity and acceleration of record accumulation. If you have the ability to configure the level or granularity of detail captured by your audit records, you may want to adjust accordingly.

- Hardware should be provisioned to accommodate growth projections of audit storage and the performance necessary to support audit operations.

- The storage and security benefits of compression and encryption standards should be weighed against any attendant usability impacts.

- Long-term storage plans should factor in all relevant growth aspects, including user and data volume expansion, as well as a plan for increased sophistication in the types of monitored user interactions as the systems evolves over time.

Retrievability

Audit logs are of little use if the logs cannot be readily accessed and efficiently analyzed. Retrievability is a requirement that is sometimes in tension with many of the others (e.g., scale, security, and format), but is nonetheless an essential consideration that motivates a careful balancing of other demands.

For example, incredibly verbose and massive audit records that are contextually augmented to be made more comprehensible to auditors and encrypted to ensure secure storage may become unwieldy to decrypt, search, and return. However, with appropriate planning and resource allocation, sensible methods can be adapted to minimize retrieval latency and other factors that might limit the efficient utilization of audit records.

To ensure retrievable audit trails, it's important to establish an effective and reliable search-and-retrieval framework. Several features help make this possible. It helps to ensure that audit records are cleanly and consistently structured, and parseable. This consistent structure does not preclude having both highly structured and constrained data fields (like usernames and IP addresses) and variable length, unstructured text fields (like typed notes, record contents, etc.). Rather, having a consistent structure allows audit records to leverage other commodity capabilities in support of efficient recall and filtering. For the structured data in an audit record, indexes predicated on commonly queried audit fields (e.g., usernames) should be constructed to enable fast retrieval of specific records, and, more importantly, filtering of large sets of records.

Retrievability is not just about finding records that might be relevant to an investigation, but also being able to filter out records that mask the relevant ones (remember, the sheer volume of audit data that even a single user may generate in one day of work can be unwieldy for human analysis). When working with unstructured data fields, use readily available search-and-retrieval technologies like search engines or full-text-indexing capabilities in traditional databases to efficiently find relevant records based on keyword searching.

Finally, the architect of your audit infrastructure should provide some clean, integrated layer to query and present the results, unifying access to the various querying-infrastructure components that support the audit workflows. A conceptual end goal should be to translate dense outputs like the one shown in Figure 9-3 into something simpler.

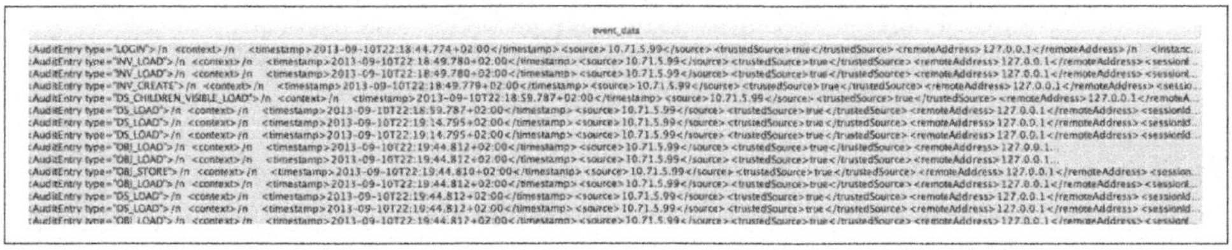

Figure 9-3. In raw form, common audit records consist of dense, poorly-formatted text that has little practical utility.

Figure 9-4 shows the result: a structured, cleanly formatted, human-readable output.

Timestamp	User	User Jurisdiction	Event/Action	Data Field	Data Source
8/19/2014 9:50	User SK254	Agency A	Login	N/A	N/A
8/29/2014 10:04	User SK254	Agency A	Search	Record 312	System X
8/29/2014 12:05	User SK254	Agency A	Export	Record 312	System X
8/29/2014 17:53	User SK254	Agency A	Create Histogram	Record 312	System Y
8/30/2014 0:38	User SK254	Agency A	Logout	N/A	N/A

Figure 9-4. Retrievable audit records should be cleanly structured for ease of viewing, sorting, and basic analysis. Auditors should, at the minimum, be able to call up a tabular view that doesn't require further scrubbing or processing in order to read and make sense of the records.

An even better translation is user-friendly conceptual representations that can be explored and analyzed in much the same way that core information systems are intended to support user analytics, like Figure 9-5.

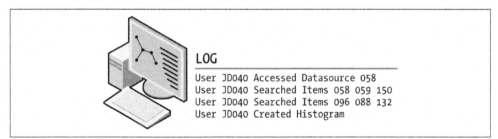

```
LOG
User JD040 Accessed Datasource 058
User JD040 Searched Items 058 059 150
User JD040 Searched Items 096 088 132
User JD040 Created Histogram
```

Figure 9-5. Retrievability should ultimately be about more than ease of searching and reading of records. Effective audit analysis may require that that auditors have the tools to visualize and manipulate the audit records using advanced methods that better expose patterns and signals indicative of misuse.

Security

The traditional role of security is to prevent unauthorized access to data, and audit records are no exception. Since audit logs may often contain copies of the sensitive data that the system houses, they will need at least as much information security as the main data system itself. In addition to including time-stamped versions of privileged data elements, audit logs may contain a trail of highly sensitive modifications to those elements, including details regarding the deletion of elements that are no longer in any way accessible within the information system proper. In this way, security administrators or others with oversight responsibility may find it necessary to recursively apply even more stringent access-control rules to audit records than would be applied to the primary data sources.

Moreover, since audit logs are intended to provide the final and canonical validation of the effective application of other privacy-protective elements of a system, their security must be of paramount concern. Given the role that auditing plays in guaranteeing the proper and sanctioned use of the system, a second-but-equally-important consideration is that audit records must rigorously resist any attempts to be modified or deleted. Put another way, if the auditing records for your system can be changed without detection, auditing no longer provides any useful guarantee about the proper use or misuse of the system. As such, the ability to provide irreproachable guarantees of audit-record soundness should be regarded as a cornerstone of an effective audit framework.

Standard methods of implementing encryption in transit and at rest (as discussed in Chapter 4) provide some assurances for audit records as they are transported and stored, and help address our first concern. However, it's the nature of the audit log to serve as a continuously amended record, and it is the act of frequent addition that introduces a notable security vulnerability related to our second concern. If the integrity of audit-log additions cannot be assured, the fidelity and reliability of audit content may not hold up to later scrutiny.

In a perfect world, audit-log administrators would be able assert the *immutability* of audit records. However, this is something of a false aspiration because, as noted in Chapter 4, no security measures are foolproof, and even the most advanced encryption techniques have vulnerabilities (peripheral to the security of the encryption algorithms themselves) under conditions of total system compromise. Without immutable audit logs, administrators may be tempted by the notion of *tamper-proof* or *tamper-resistant* logs. But this is also a false aspiration because the necessary ability is to *demonstrably assert* the integrity of audit logs—a tampered audit log can be made to look as pure and clean as one might believe an unsullied audit log ought to look. The security outcome administrators and architects should aspire to bring about the notion of *tamper evidence*. This is the idea that the integrity of audit trails can be assured such that even if a nefarious, malevolent, evil super-genius hacker *could* in principle, with all stars aligned, "break into" the audit trails and alter them, she would not be able to do so without introducing some easily detectable trace.

One method of implementing *tamper-evident* logs is called *cryptographic hash-chaining* (see sidebar). This technique creates a cryptographic link between each entry and makes any changes, removals, or additions to the log readily detectable.

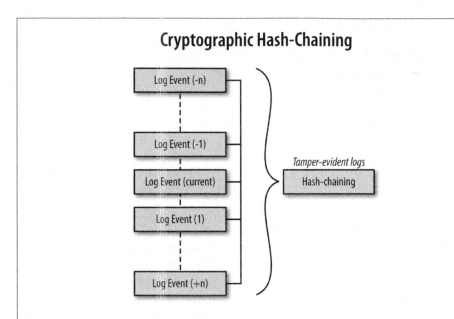

Cryptographic Hash-Chaining

Log Event (-n)

Log Event (-1)

Log Event (current)

Log Event (1)

Log Event (+n)

Tamper-evident logs

Hash-chaining

When dealing with a single message, a common technique to guarantee that the message has not been altered is to use a *hash-based message authentication code* or *HMAC*. It's sometimes also referred to as a *cryptographic signature* or just a *signature*. The action of generating an HMAC for a piece of data is often called *signing*, as it produces a piece of data called a signature—and like a traditional signature, it can be used to verify the integrity and source of the data.

Conceptually, an HMAC is generated by combining a secret key with the message data and then generating a cryptographically-secure hash of the combined data.[1] HMACs have a couple of important features:

- The hash function will generate a different hash code for any modification of the message, such that any modification of the message will cause a verification check of the message using the HMAC.

- Valid HMACs can only be generated by a process that is in possession of the secret key, foiling anyone *not* in possession of the key that attempts to generate a new, valid HMAC for an altered message.

---

1 A cryptographically secure hash function is one that, like all hash functions, will produce a fixed-length output based on a variable-length input with a low probability of collision on its expected range of inputs. To be cryptographically secure, it must be practically irreversible—i.e., it must be impossible to derive the input data from the hash output and have a probability of collision that approaches zero.

In practice, HMACs are very useful for protecting individual messages from alteration or forgery. However, in the case of audit logging, this alone is not sufficient. While it's important that each individual log entry be verifiable, the integrity of the audit log depends on no messages being omitted from the audit log. One can imagine an attacker performing a nefarious action and then simply erasing the portion of the audit log that recorded the action. In such an instance, all the remaining entries in the audit log would still verify as genuine, but the log itself would have been compromised.

To solve this problem, a technique called hash-chaining can be used, in which the generation of the HMAC for each entry requires a third piece of information: the hash of the previous entry in the log. The secret key, the message itself, and the HMAC from the previous entry area are all combined to generate the HMAC. To aid in the verification of individual entries, a traditional HMAC (using only the message and secret key) can also be recorded with each entry. This obviates the need to verify the entire chain of entries in the log to validate one individual entry, though it may serve as a useful optimization, trading space in the log for runtime performance of verification.

Hash-chaining guards against the removal of entries from the log, such that an undetected removal of a single entry would necessitate rewriting every subsequent entry in the log. Since rewriting an entry requires the secret key, as long as the secret key is properly protected, hash-chaining makes logs *tamper-evident*.

If a secret key is compromised, an attacker could rewrite the entire audit log, effectively erasing their tracks and *leaving no trace that the log had ever been altered*. Given that no security mechanism is perfectly foolproof, further steps can be taken to ensure that any changes made to the audit log can be detected.

One technique to detect when a log has been altered via secret-key compromise is to use an external authority as a checkpoint for the HMAC chain using cryptographic signatures. Periodically, an HMAC in the chain is sent to what is called a *timestamp service*.[2]. The timestamp service creates its own HMAC using a different, and more carefully controlled, private key. That signature is then stored in the hash chain along with the timestamp of when the entry was submitted. Then, when verifying the log entries, the timestamp service's signature is also verified against its public key. Therefore, even if an attacker should happen to gain control of the audit process's secret key, the attacker will not be able to generate new signatures from the timestamp service and the additional entries will be more readily identifiable as fakes. The benefit here is that an attacker who compromises the secret key can only alter or fake the entries since the last timestamp service signature was received and written to the log.

Timestamp services are fairly straightforward services to build and operate, and there are many commercial implementations upon which to draw when constructing your

---

2 Wikipedia has a good overview of timestamp services (*http://bit.ly/wiki-timestamp*).

tamper-evident auditing system. The most important aspect of these services is to make sure they are very difficult to compromise. One method for mitigating the risk of the service being compromised though physical tampering is to use a *hardware security module* (HSM)—a specialized piece of hardware used to store cryptographic keys and perform cryptographic processing. However, one drawback to introducing a timestamp service into a logging architecture is that it introduces a new piece of key infrastructure that may complicate the operation of the overall system. As with every technology and strategy discussed in this book, the complexities and costs of implementing cryptographic hash-chaining as a method of securing audit logs should be weighed against the overall requirements and goals for your product.

Access Control

To support additional, layered security on audit retrieval and analysis, the audit system should further allow for a complex authorization model drawing upon some of the access-control principles addressed in Chapter 6. There are a few related requirements of such a model worth considering:

- Different auditors may have variable access to user information
- Access should be overseen by a supervisor or high-level owner
- Auditor permissions should be flexible enough to change over time, including supporting permission modifications and access revocation when no longer needed
- Auditors should be granted timely, temporary permission to perform investigations on specific subsets of the auditing data, rather than wholesale access to all auditing data

Depending on how your organization's oversight authorities are structured, you may wish to consider adapting to one of the following auditing regime configurations:

- All auditors see everything
- Some auditors see everything; others see only a subset of data
- Auditors have a fine-grained set of permissions that control what can and cannot be seen
- Build and support discovery permissions within audit records[3]

The above options should seem familiar, as they are ways to apply the same privacy protections outlined before—no more, no less. Instead of limiting access and expo-

---

3 See Chapter 6 for more on discovery permissions.

sure to the original sensitive data itself, we are applying those limitations to a form of metadata: the auditing data that describes how the original data has been used (which incidentally may also include views of the data itself).

Retention

Sensible retention and purging policies and practices should be adopted for audit data. When designing your policy, it's worth considering the intention and purpose of both the audit-retention policy and how it interacts with the policies for the original data. While initially it may seem prudent to retain *all* audit logs indefinitely, this may be undesirable for a number of reasons. For example:

- Given that audit records can grow at a rapid clip, the purging of audit logs can help mitigate issues around the scale of auditing data, although it will entail some sacrifices in losing the complete historical record of how the system has been used.

- From a security perspective, the indefinite retention of audit records will increase information security risk by creating an additional set of perpetually growing sensitive records that need to be protected.

- When a piece of data is purged from the main system, should its associated audit records also be purged?

- Should an audit-log entry documenting the purging of a record itself be purged or retained? On the one hand, retaining the audit record serves as proof of the mandated deletion. On the other hand, if the intention of purging is to remove any record that the data ever existed, the existence of an audit record that acknowledges the previous existence of the data (even without containing the original data) may be problematic.

- Does the audit record itself hold any of the original data intended to be deleted? If audit records are being retained indefinitely, it is literally impossible to ever truly purge data from the system.

Audit Logging and the Fair Information Practice Principles (FIPPs)

Insofar as other privacy-enhancing features manifest the various FIPPs, audit logging also encompasses those principles by acting as their guarantor. The entire point of audit logging and analysis is to validate the use, efficacy, and proper functioning of all other privacy-protective measures. For example, the principles of *Purpose Specification* and *Use Limitation*, as instantiated through the use of access controls and selective revelation measures, may be fully implemented and work exactly as intended, but unless there is some record of those measures in use, the proper functioning and efficacy of these privacy-enhancing features may be subject to doubt. Auditing therefore implies responsibility. It provides a framework for enabling accountability and oversight of system use—and it is the only way to guarantee that access to sensitive information is not being improperly used or intentionally abused without anyone's knowledge.

Advanced Auditing Considerations

Much of what has been described thus far in the chapter provides an important framework and infrastructure for building baseline auditing systems and best practices. With those elements in place, a world of advanced auditing prospects is made available. Auditing is in many ways nothing other than a way of analyzing data, and so many of the advanced tools and considerations that constitute powerful information systems can also be turned to the problem of understanding audit records. But audit logging as an information system function should still be regarded as a critical capability that must be protected, preserved, and itself subject to review in order to serve as a reliable guarantor of all of the other features you may built and deployed in making a privacy-protective system.

Reactive Versus Proactive Auditing

Most discussion around audit logs refers to reactive auditing. For example, after a system is breached, administrators and investigators will turn to the audit logs for retrospective understanding of what went wrong. This type of auditing is reminiscent of forensic inquiry. Investigative effort is directed at methodically reconstructing any aberrations, failings, or abuse. Problems that are identified are subsequently addressed by fixing the vulnerabilities, providing restitution to those who may have been harmed or put at risk by the unwarranted exposure, and possibly dealing with the personnel involved. But the starting point for reactive auditing is always a known incident.

However, many of the considerations outlined above can be applied to proactive auditing as well. Proactive auditing focuses on signaling risky user behaviors or system activity as it is occurring. Behavior monitors using simple pattern matching, data mining, or even machine-learning models against the audit logs serve as near-real-time flags of concerning actions. If the audit logs are well-constructed and the infrastructure exists to support efficient processing and machine readability, "tripwires" can readily flag problematic details in the audit logs nearly as rapidly as those logs are being generated. Of course, the additional challenge in this type of application is in creating the correct proactive tripwires in the first place. However, these might be simpler rule sets defined by institutional policies such as prohibitions on working outside of standard operations hours or limitations on the volume of records to include in export events. Moreover, patterns of malfeasance identified in previous forensic-audit investigations can later be codified and programmed as proactive trip-wires for identifying similar future abuses as they happen.

Emergency Stop for Audit-Log Failures

A properly functioning audit-logging system should be a necessary requirement for the overall system to remain operational. Since in many ways, audit logging serves as the backbone of a reliable and privacy-protective system architecture, any failure of the auditing framework should halt all other operations. When audit logging breaks down, vulnerabilities, failures, and abuse can amass without any trace, creating privacy-related and other harm that will be effectively immeasurable. For this reason, safeguards should be instituted to make a failing of the audit-logging system trigger the immediate and complete cessation of, at minimum, all nonvital user-facing operations.

Audit the Auditors

The auditing patterns we've discussed in this chapter are multifaceted and complex. As with any complicated system, the more ornate the infrastructure becomes, the more risky the prospects of malicious (or nonmalicious) abuse or failure. It may be worth considering an additional level of recursive systems design to help audit the auditors and ensure that their interactions with audit logs and administration of the audit system is secure and sound.

Conclusion

Auditing is a necessary and foundational component to any trusted system. Without oversight on the access granted to users of sensitive data, there is no way to guard against abuse—abuse that may not even be imagined or enumerated at the time of system design. By starting your design with the auditing system in accordance with the principles and considerations described in this chapter, the ultimate safeguard of active monitoring by other humans is baked into your architecture. Leaving auditing as an afterthought risks invalidating all the other safeguards built into the system and can ultimately lead to systemic failure wherein even a well-constructed, privacy-protective, and seemingly accountable system can't be considered trustworthy.

CHAPTER 10

Data Retention and Data Purging

Some of us think holding on makes us strong; but sometimes it is letting go.
—Hermann Hesse

Overview

So far, we've covered approaches to retrieving, storing, accessing, and exposing data as a means of securing and protecting informational privacy. This chapter will explore what to do when data should, for various reasons, be available or retained only for a fixed period, after which availability should either be indefinitely revoked or the data itself should be purged from the system. The notion of "purging" information, which might seem straightforward in analogous paper records contexts, is quite complex in digital-storage contexts where purging practices can take on many flavors. There is a spectrum of approaches that may be taken to handle the purging of records, as well as a set of considerations to weigh in determining the optimal approach for a given set of common constraints and requirements.

What Is Data Retention?

Data retention refers to the implementation of a policy that dictates data is to be removed from a system (or at least made unavailable to general users). This policy framework generally weighs competing sets of interests. On the one hand, there may be legal, privacy, procedural, and other practical constraints (e.g., storage limitations) that militate against holding onto information. On the other hand, countervailing factors including utility, transparency, and economics may tip the scale in favor of extended data preservation. Ideally, the contextualized balancing of these competing motivations should determine the appropriate retention periods, archival rules, encryption standards, and eventual purging practices. For this reason, data retention is anything but one-size-fits-all. Rather, it is a conceptual plan encompassing a range of approaches that are best settled upon through a holistic evaluation of benefits and tradeoffs in relation to the specifics of a given data type, its origin and uses, and the broader system and enterprise in which the data resides.

Why Is Data Retention Important?

There are often a number of considerations that might motivate the adoption of data-retention policies applied to a given type of data held by an information system. These considerations may overlap and reinforce each other in numerous ways, or they also may be idiosyncratic and isolated in their application to very specific contexts. They may also be countervailing or dissonant with each other.

Legal and policy compliance

Sensitive records that are regulated by law or institutional policy frequently involve some kind of statutory maximum (and/or minimum) data-retention requirement. Records may be considered sensitive or statutorily protected because they implicate personally identifying information, assert uncertain or unverified claims, create security risks if exposed, among other reasons. In these cases, limiting the period of retention may therefore mitigate the risks of exposure. Conversely, minimum data-holding principles may be instituted as statutory requirements for auditing, oversight, and regulatory accountability reasons. For example, telecommunications and information service providers that fall under the jurisdiction of the Federal Communications Commission are required to retain call detail records for a minimum of 18 months in order to facilitate the resolution of billing disputes.[1]

Data quality

Although the digital medium is generally regarded as reliable for preserving the fidelity of data over time (in contrast to analogue-storage methods that may be prone to physical decay), the quality of data—in relation to its original collection purposes—may nonetheless erode. This is because the world that the data once represented may change in ways that undermine or invalidate the data. More recent information may come to represent a qualitative improvement over older data that perhaps represents a state of the world that no longer exists or is irrelevant. In this way, the retention of older data may actually become a risk to organizations, in that its presence muddles applications by adding clutter or noise that obfuscates or detracts from the more valuable signal. For example, a marketer might be interested in using customers' historical purchase patterns as an indicator of current retail interests. However, the historical patterns of a male col-

---

1 47 CFR § 42.6 requires that, "[e]ach carrier that offers or bills toll telephone service shall retain for a period of 18 months such records as are necessary to provide . . . billing information . . .."

lege student may change once he enters the workforce, marries, and starts a family—all within the span of a couple of years. Continuing to rely on earlier information for modeling his consumption habits without appropriately retiring data that has aged beyond its time of use will produce qualitatively undesirable results.

Resource constraints

It is well understood that information-storage costs have continually declined for most of the computer age and that they are likely to continue that trajectory for some time still as storage-technology advances continue apace. For many organizations with limited resources, however, the velocity of data collection may still outpace cost decreases, eventually leading to capacity limitations. At the risk of having systems fail under critical operational circumstances, protocols may be adopted to systemically cull data deemed irrelevant, outdated, or unnecessary so as to free up storage space.

Protection against repurposing

A common temptation with data collected for a given objective is that it may later be discovered to hold additional value that falls far afield of the initial purpose. For example, it might be necessary to hold on to telephone company communication records in order to help resolve billing disputes, but these might later on prove useful for marketing purposes. This type of repurposing is particularly problematic when it undermines the terms provided to data subjects at the point of initial collection. Had consumers known of the eventual uses, they might not have consented to having their data collected in the first place. By voluntarily adopting a retention policy, systems can impose constraints that limit these risks by avoiding the temptation altogether and constraining the data scope to focus on the use cases for which it was initially gathered.

Efficiency requirements

As systems amass data (and particularly data types that carry certain sensitivities such as classification levels or that are personally identifying), certain needs may also accumulate in ways that generate unmanageable inefficiencies. For example, historical data may have curation or vetting requirements that become increasingly unwieldy for larger data sets. Alternatively, very massive data scales may introduce computational challenges that make working with the data increasingly inefficient or costly. Paring down data may, in such cases, serve as a sensible method for minimizing such challenges.

Privacy protection

Privacy interests may dictate a policy of limited retention—in this case, privacy in the guise of giving individuals an escape from an indelible past. Much has been made recently, for example, of the so-called "Right to be forgotten," under which individuals can demand that information about them be deleted from a data set not in their control. Were such a right to be widely adopted—either by legislative fiat, market pressures, or some combination of the two—individuals would be able to assert greater control over their data, thereby allowing greater ability to "edit" their lives as recorded and processed by others.

But beyond just excising embarrassing party photos or expunging an arrest record, the power to delete may implicate something far more significant. In some ways, the right to forget is a legislative means of imposing a digital analogue to the normative functioning of memory, which decays over time and allows future prospects to open up less hindered by and subject to individuals' pasts. In the modern world of digital information, the enduring fidelity of digital media is one of its greatest virtues—as well as potentially its greatest curse. The fear that a record about one's historical self will forever haunt him or her becomes a matter of self-determination. Here, privacy becomes a means to the end of having the freedom to evolve and to reinvent oneself free of the damning imprint of an inescapable digital record. Consequently, this conception of privacy demands that records should be actively purged after a certain period of time to prevent the prospects of abuse, repurposing, or simply resurfacing details of a life that no longer meaningfully reflect the true person.

These considerations are rarely mutually exclusive and often codependent. For example, a regulatory requirement for the retention of a particular data type may have originally been motivated by policymakers' concerns about the quality of a noisy, poorly collected, questionably maintained data source, or out of privacy interests articulated on behalf of the underlying data subjects. Similarly, a massive and unpruned data source may create efficiency challenges in processing due to resource constraints such as insufficient storage or computing power. The compounding of reasons should only serve to elevate the importance of addressing data retention. Whatever the reason or reasons for considering a data-retention policy, it is important to anticipate these requirements as much as possible when developing a system's architecture so that the technical capabilities needed to effectively manage the retaining or purging of information are in place when needed.

How to Set Retention and Purge Policies

In order to codify retention policies and implement them in a system, you'll need to understand the underlying motivations behind them (such as the considerations articulated above). You'll also need to evaluate your fixed and nonnegotiable resource constraints, as well as the optional and negotiable ones, and their corresponding trade-offs with your intended policies.

Legal requirements should prevail over all other potentially conflicting considerations. Where laws or policies dictate the retention or purging of records, they should be faithfully followed in letter and spirit. Failure to observe the law may lead to compliance sanctions, or worse. Even where compliance may incur significant additional cost (in monetary or performance terms), operating in violation of the law should not be entertained as an option.

If organizations can find locally determined reasons to "overachieve" with respect to statutory requirements, they should consider doing so. Legal standards for records retention and purging often take rounded numbers (e.g., a five-year maximum retention rule for criminal intelligence files for law enforcement agencies under 28 Code of Federal Regulation [CFR] Part 23; a six-year minimum retention requirement for medical documentation under Health Insurance Portability and Accountability Act of 1996 [HIPAA]). But these specific numbers may be somewhat arbitrary, grounded more in the need to select some reasonable threshold or limit that stakeholders can agree to in principle, rather than any rigorous evaluation or theory. It's probably wise to regard these legal retention and purging requirements as minimum thresholds or limits to be met, and exceed their spirit in practice. This is especially true with regard to data purging. If records are being held until a statutorily specified maximum time period, even though they've lost their utility and value well before then and have no compelling reason for not being subjected to a more aggressive purge schedule, then an earlier purge standard is likely the more prudent course.

Where existing laws or policy do not impose clear retention burdens, it often makes sense to consider other practical constraints and considerations in formulating an *elective* retention policy. Questions to consider in this regard might be:

What's the shelf-life of the data?
    In other words, when does the data cease to be useful or appreciably degrade in quality? This is often a question that can only be answered empirically, and any available historical evidence or analysis may serve well as a guide for formulating a retention standard. For example, by looking at the historical usage of retained data and evaluating the most common age at which the utility and usage of older data appears to most sharply drop off, you may be able to determine a very sensible, data-driven standard for a self-imposed retention policy.

What are the risks/rewards of indefinite retention?
    Understanding whether prolonged retention is likely to create additional liabilities, such as expanded scope in data-breach exposure, is important to weigh against any presumed upsides of holding the data (e.g., potential or previously unimagined analysis use cases). Conversely, if extended data retention is likely to preserve and later make available important exculpatory evidence, then that should also be balanced against the advantages of an earlier deletion plan.

What costs will be incurred by needlessly holding on to data?
    Particularly in systems and enterprises where indefinite data retention is liable to strain the computing or storage capacities of hardware, it's worth evaluating

whether the expenses associated with scaling machinery are truly justifiable and sustainable in the long term given reasonable data-growth projections.

If your only compelling rationale for justifying the indefinite holding of data is the vague belief that the data may some day acquire some previously unknown value, then that's probably a sound indication to consider a voluntary retention policy. Often, this line of reasoning lubricates a slippery slope into scope creep through the nebulous hope that data might eventually take on value beyond the purposes for which it was originally acquired. The ubiquity and questionable grounding of justifying indefinite data retention based on the prospect that the data may eventually "come in handy" has led to heightened scrutiny of organizations that draw upon this justification. It's worth evaluating whether the reputational risks associated with such a data-retention motive are worth defending against in the court of public opinion.

So You Want to Purge Data. Now What?

The decision to purge information is not as simple as it sounds. Appropriate methods may vary according to institutional constraints, the need to balance against reporting requirements, efficacy considerations, and prevailing interpretations of information-retrievability risks. Even in the loosely analogous paper-records paradigm, institutions faced with purging information may explore a range of options including redaction of personally identifying or sensitive information fields (i.e., blacking out of certain text elements while preserving the document as a whole); moving the document to a more restricted filing or storage facility; or shredding, pulping, immolating, or otherwise physically destroying the document. In more modern digital-information systems, the gamut of choices for implementing purging are even more expansive and run an even broader range of methods of variable complexity, completeness, permanency, and retrievability.

We might broadly divide the various possible purging strategies into nondeletion purging and deletion purging (see Figure 10-1, which shows gradations of purge techniques and corresponding degrees of retrievability). The primary distinction is that the former entails some level of preservation and retrievability of records (though they may forever be limited to a very narrow group of viewers), while the latter entails degrees of deletion or destruction of records such that records become effectively or actually irretrievable.

Nondeletion Purging (or Not-Quite-Gone)

Purging information doesn't necessarily imply that the data is completely destroyed, or made inaccessible and irretrievable to all users for all time. In fact, there are a host of methods for systems that, for whatever reason, require a lighter approach to purging.

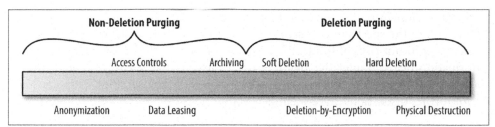

Figure 10-1. Purging techniques run the gamut from partial reduction to physical destruction. At one end of the spectrum, nondeletion-purging methods may be reversible, making information retrievable albeit with increasing effort. Toward the other end of the spectrum, deletion-purging methods are increasingly more difficult to reverse, making purged data gone for good.

Partial redaction

Some information regimes call for partial redaction of sensitive records' fields in order to de-identify the record. This essentially involves obscuring from view certain components or sub-components of a record that might, if present, be deemed personally identifying, restricted, classified, or otherwise sensitive. In obscuring its sensitive elements, the remaining record is therefore determined to be exempt from more onerous, lasting, and complete purge requirements. For example, a record that contains identifying information, billing information, and a list of health conditions is considered a medical record and subject to certain special handling rules. But if the health conditions are redacted, then the record is no longer a medical record and those rules no longer apply.

Anonymization

Anonymization is somewhat similar to redaction except that it only relates to sub-components of information that are personally identifying information. Anonymization involves stripping or obscuring personally identifying information fields of records from the view of nonprivileged end users. For example, a spreadsheet containing a list of individuals with their Name, Age, and Gender is anonymized if the Name column (the only column that makes a one-to-one identification with a real individual) is removed.

Related to anonymization is pseudonymization, which involves removing the identifying information and replacing those fields with, for example, an identification number or other tag. In pseudonymizing data in this way, records continue to assert the uniqueness of the actual thing to which they correspond but no longer are ostensibly associated with that thing. In order to pseudonymize the spreadsheet described above, instead of eliminating the Name column altogether, each name is replaced with a unique but random sequence of characters that will persist with the data set.

Redaction, anonymization, and pseudonymization approaches to purging fall at the lighter end of the spectrum because they are both minimally destructive *and* also can present significant risks of re-identification or drawing on the preserved and exposed information fields to infer the identities or reconstruct the sensitive elements of the data that was intended to be obscured from the view of the user. (See Chapters 2 and 11 for further discussions on re-identification.)

A Word on Anonymization, Aggregate Statistics, and Differential Privacy

Anonymization techniques are often employed as a preliminary step to generating aggregate statistics. These statistics are often intended to provide summary insights abstracted from any particular or identifying detail of an underlying data element. Anonymization and aggregation can also serve as a pipeline for data purging whereby purged data lives on only in the reduced form of some set of aggregate measures (e.g., grouped sums, averages, or other common statistic). In either case, the idea is that the data provides some enduring utility in a de-identified or higher-level form. The fundamental privacy challenge with aggregate statistics used to generate de-identified insights or enduring records is that they can all too readily be re-identified.[2]

One emerging area of research into privacy-protective systems is an idea called *differential privacy*, which is concerned with understanding the risk of re-identification inherent in a set of aggregate statistics. The basic idea is that, through a pattern of queries, it's possible to identify information about individuals in a dataset that appears to be anonymized. Differential privacy is a set of techniques designed to measure the privacy risks associated with a given query and, where there exists an unacceptable risk of re-identification, inject noise into the data set to more adequately mask information about individuals. The central question that differential privacy concerns itself with is the differential risk created by the addition or removal of a single record with regards to re-identification. Each query is given a measure of re-identification risk; when that risk exceeds some desired threshold, the system injects noise randomly drawn from Laplace distribution that matches the underlying data involved in the query.

It's a technique that's very popular in academic circles, as it places formal measures on the question of privacy risk. From an analytical perspective, it presents clean algorithms for preserving privacy in statistical databases. In practice, differential privacy is not a panacea. First of all, it's only applicable to databases presenting aggregate statistics—meaning that it is of no utility in situations where individual records will be accessed. Second, in practice, creating that risk measure can be a difficult process to

---

2 See Paul Ohm's "Broken Promises of Privacy: Responding to the Surprising Failure of Anonymization" (*http://bit.ly/ohms-broken-promises*).

get right. Finally, for certain types of distributions, notably computations of averages that contain large outliers, the injection of noise necessary to make differential privacy work can distort results to the point of absurdity.

Given the energy behind differential privacy as a practice, it's likely to be increasingly applied to certain types of systems. However, although its formal measures and guarantees are attractive properties in privacy engineering, the shortcomings of differential privacy will likely mean its use will be limited. Insofar as differential privacy may apply to addressing data-purging requirements, it, like most other statistical measures, will likely serve as more of a method for information insights to live on in some aggregated form after a robust purging method has been applied.

Access controls

Access controls provide great flexibility in ensuring that only those who have a legitimate right to know sensitive data will have access to it (for more information, see Chapter 6). Just as access controls can be used to restrict information according to permission groups, they can also be applied as granular tools for placing sensitive data entirely beyond the reach of users to serve as a makeshift purge mechanism. With this method, the more restrictive the membership of the corresponding access group, the more inaccessible that information becomes and may therefore qualify as being purged.

Data leasing

A data lease, or a time-based access control, makes it possible to mark a subset of sensitive data as restricted, but still gives some users unrestricted access to that data for a limited time. In a data-leasing setup, users can request access to restricted data and administrators can "lease" the data to them, setting a time when the lease will expire and the data will once again become restricted and inaccessible to the users who previously leased it. To regain access, a user would need to request a new lease. Depending on the sensitivity of the data being used, it may also make sense to give users the power to mark or nominate existing or new data to be restricted if it had not been previously marked as such when it should have been. This builds in an additional corrective mechanism to improve data protection over time.

Different kinds of users may require different kinds of data leases. Some users may need the ability to discover that restricted data exists, judge that it might be relevant to their work, and request access from data owners and administrators. Some users might be assigned to be part of a work group that will operate for six months and needs access to a certain data source for that period but not beyond it. The permutations can be as nuanced as your system requires. (For more information on time-based access controls, see Chapter 6.)

Archiving

Archiving is a method of removing data from normal usage by stripping access and cordoning off data to a more secure and restrictive storage environment. In this method, the data still persists in its complete form but is effectively cut off from retrieval by nonadministrative users. Archiving data may involve removing the data from a system's underlying database transactional tables and then blocking it off to separate backup tables for an appropriate span of time. By archiving data, it's possible to reproduce data when required (e.g., in a legal proceeding) while keeping it out of the reach of system users who have no real need to have access to it. Users only work with the nonarchived operational data.

Archiving data also brings additional positive outcomes unrelated to privacy and data stewardship. By actively reducing the amount of information retained on transactional database tables, the operational system will tend to perform better and incur less hardware costs over time.

There's a range of different methods for making data inaccessible, yet still preserved indefinitely in some form or other. These methods may be sufficient for purging in certain environments but not in others, especially those dictated by law or regulation. However, redacted, anonymized, access-restricted, leased, or archived data may still resurface in unwanted ways—for example, through residual data traces,[3] imperfect technical implementations, or security breaches. They may therefore be undesirable for organizations concerned with having to respond to third-party subpoena requests, for which it's qualitatively distinct to respond, "these records no longer exist" as opposed to "nobody is permitted to look at these records in our systems." Such risks may be intolerable in certain situations and therefore warrant more final purging methods. In short, while nondeletion purge techniques (like access controls, archiving, etc.) are useful and practical in some cases, there are deep and qualitative differences from more complete deletion and purging techniques.

---

3 Residual data traces may result from a common database principle of referential integrity, which holds that references across an information store should be valid and intact. When, for example, purging in one table of a database fails to cascade to other linked tables or components, the "dangling references" create potential data leaks of sensitive information. For example, a deleted user in a system may have sent messages to other users, received messages from them, or engaged in transactions with them (such as buying or selling something, rating them, being rated by them, responding to their comments on a forum, giving them objects or resources within a video game, etc.). That history is "about" the deleted user, but it's also "about" other users who continue to exist within the system, and may be necessary in order to make those users' experiences, records, or statistics make sense. This can also affect organizations trying to purge information about former employees: records that indicate that certain employees took particular actions on particular occasions won't make sense. For what it's worth, these issues are easiest to solve with log-style records that don't explicitly have any kind of cross-referencing. Most organizations could easily delete their old server logs without breaking anything, unless they've somehow pulled them into a database that's started generating cross-references on top of the logs. For more, see Michael Blaha, "Referential Integrity Is Important For Databases" (*http://bit.ly/blaha-referential*).

Deletion Purging (or Gradations of Gone)

Deletion purging methods are intended to make undesirable data retrieval much harder (or even impossible) by applying more irreversible methods. These don't just rigorously enforce inaccessibility but permanently destroy or delete the information altogether. In this context, *deletion* connotes clearing a subset of memory or storage space of the data it once held and freeing it up for new data. There are a number of variations of deletion, which implicate varying degrees of finality.

Soft deletion

In "soft" deletion, records are effectively removed from end-user access via *frontend* applications, but could (at least temporarily and with some nonnegligible effort) be retrieved by *backend* systems administrators. In a technical sense, soft deletion typically involves the act of designating memory or storage space that holds the purged information available for overwriting. Eventually, through ordinary system usage, new data will be written over the old data, after which it will be truly irretrievable. In the meantime, until new data is written to that site, the old data remains in place, though it is harder to access (since its address in the system's file system directory or the pointer to the relevant disk sector is what actually moved, not the data itself). This phenomenon, in which nominally deleted data is actually still stored for a time and can, with effort and the right instruments, be retrieved, is called *data remanence*.

For lighter privacy policies, soft deletion might be sufficient. It may even be preferable if there are requirements to restore data using un-deletion utilities or computer forensics tools that can directly read from storage disk sectors and get at the old data that remains in place. However, for more stringent requirements, a more comprehensive approach to dealing with remnant data may be necessary.

Deletion-by-encryption

Encryption can be repurposed to enhance privacy. Typically, when we encrypt data, we do it with the intention of decrypting it again in the future. For this reason, we keep the encryption key. However, if we want to put the data beyond reach, we could also choose to encrypt that data and destroy the encryption key, which is known as "bricking" the data as ciphertext for the foreseeable future. Similar to "soft" deletion, the data is still in place on a system somewhere, but in an unreadable form.

Encryption can function as a check on third parties to which we might not want to give total trust. While this might seem like a strange approach, consider a situation in which a user wants to deactivate or delete a particular account, and has the ability to encrypt the data previously shared. By being the only one in control of the encryption key—and choosing to destroy that key—the user has greater assurance that the company is not surreptitiously still holding and using the data even after it was instructed to be removed. This way, even if the company is dishonest and doesn't actually delete the user's account and information, the company won't be able to make use of it because the data is unreadable.

An alternative implementation of this approach is to encrypt the relevant data with a randomly generated key that neither the user nor the system stores. The data is unreadable by any user the instant it is encrypted. This method is sometimes called *crypto erase* or *cryptographic disk erasure*.

In these implementations of deletion-by-encryption, the encrypting of storage media and the restricting or destruction of encryption keys enforces the notion of the encrypted records becoming *effectively* irretrievable to undesired parties. Deletion-by-encryption is seen increasingly as a more viable alternative to the more extreme deletion options applied to cloud-hosted environments, where physical destruction is simply not a viable option.

Hard delete

A stricter requirement may necessitate the immediate overwriting of all bits containing purged records both in memory and storage. "Hard" delete typically refers to methods of deletion whereby all frontend *and* backend accessible versions of data have been destroyed and retrieval is no longer possible by any means. There are different purging techniques for implementing hard delete, but they all have the goal of making it virtually impossible to reconstitute or retrieve the purged data.

Small-scale hard deletions involve irreversibly removing a record or designated set of records from database tables and stored search indexes, while leaving other undesignated data intact. Other hard-delete techniques, such as data wiping and overwriting, are more expansive. They write a pattern of several passes of new data over the entire storage space and then verify that the old data is gone. There are several accepted standards for data wiping, which is often used to purge an entire hard disk. A hard delete can seem extreme, but it is very useful if you find your system storing sensitive data that it shouldn't be storing or where policies dictate a firm notion of data irretrievability.

Physical hardware destruction

When methodically overwriting or flipping bits is not enough, more drastic measures involving the functional or actual destruction of hardware may be required.[4] More

---

4 Simply discarding hardware is insufficient to sanitize sensitive information, and systems architects relying on external vendors for hardware disposal services should strongly consider deletion-by-encryption or hard deletion prior to relinquishing hardware. For example, see Simson L. Garfinkel and Abhi Shelat, "Remembrance of Data Passed: A Study of Disk Sanitization Practices" (*http://bit.ly/garfinkel-disk-sanitization*). While some of the hard drives in the experiment had seen attempts to delete their contents, in many cases these attempts didn't work at all and the data was largely or fully recoverable.

---

moderate forms of physical destruction include magnetic data deletion, or *degaussing*. Degaussing reduces or entirely removes the storage hardware's magnetic field, which completely eliminates the data stored on the drive. Degaussing, however, may be ineffective on certain types of storage devices such as solid state drives (SSDs). Particular storage media or rigorous policy environments may therefore require extreme physical destruction techniques (e.g., shredding, incinerating, corroding, melting, dissolving, irradiating) as more reliable approaches to putting that data securely beyond reach.[5]

Physical hardware destruction, while serving as the most complete and irreversible method of data purging, is also often the least desirable method because of the costs incurred. Hardware that has been destroyed in this manner can no longer be used and must be replaced (and at not-inconsiderable expense). This method is often a last resort, or reserved for environments with grave data sensitivities for which no other deletion method is deemed adequate. It can also be more appropriate as a data-security measure to safeguard sensitive data at the end of the hardware's life cycle. However, it remains the strongest way to circumvent misuse or abuse of data.

Practical Steps of Data Retention

Having settled on an appropriate deletion standard for your system, you'll need to ensure your data-management plan includes a handful of key practices. Good data-retention implementations begin with good data curation. Without a methodical and carefully planned process for assigning basic metadata to help track the lineage of data fields, implementing retention standards or strategies can be daunting. At minimum, records metadata should include a cluster of basic data properties, such as:

- The record's creation date
- The date of the event associated with the record (if applicable)
- The date of the most recent modification of the record
- The date on which the record may be subject to purging

Additionally, there should be some clear and unequivocal method used to distinguish those records subject to retention standards from those that are not. This can involve something as simple as a single binary property tag denoting whether the record should be considered under the applicable purge policy. It could also be something more sophisticated, such as enabling a multistakeholder, multicriteria vetting process that culminates with the annotation of the purging (or retention) decision and any supporting details, justifications, and/or authorizations.

---

5 See the NIST Guidelines for Media Sanitization (*http://bit.ly/nist-media-sanitization*).

Basic metadata curation of information systems records is essential to transacting an appropriate data-purging protocol. Figure 10-2 provides a basic outline of what these metadata fields might include in various records contexts.

Field	Call Record	Police Record	Medical Record
Creation Date	2012-02-01 22:50	2014-09-04 00:21	1980-07-19 05:21
Event Date - Start	2012-02-01 22:43	2014-09-03 20:45	1980-07-19 00:17
Event Date - End	2012-02-01 22:49	2014-09-03 22:00	1980-07-19 05:17
Last Modification Date	2012-02-01 22:50	2015-03-01 09:31	1980-07-19 05:21
Created By	John Q. Public	Officer Smith	Dr. Jones
Is Eligible for Purge	Yes	Yes	No
Purge Date	2018-02-01 22:49	2019-09-03 20:45	N/A
Notation	NULL	Criminal Intelligence	NULL

Figure 10-2. Basic metadata curation of information systems records is essential to transacting an appropriate data-purging protocol.

Instituting this class of practical measures upfront can carry a number of benefits. This type of metadata allows systems administrators and oversight authorities to more thoroughly track data life-cycle events and better understand how users interact with system data. Such knowledge can help them to make better data-retention decisions by potentially identifying users whose workflows might be critically affected by those decisions and providing them with the opportunity to justify data-retention extensions. More generally, this metadata helps them to understand the pedigree and the age of every piece of data in the system, potentially providing insight that can help make other data-driven decisions related to adopting (additional) self-governance standards easier.

There are many metadata elements that could be associated with records, so a balance between essential curation and other practical constraints is necessary. Providing too much detail on data lineage as it relates to all user interactions with the data might, for example, risk a ballooning of metadata, which may undermine the efficiency and cost motivations that warranted the adoption of the retention policy in the first place. You should also factor such overhead considerations into your initial cost-benefit analysis and retention-policy implementation plan.

Data Retention, Purging, and the FIPPs

Data retention policies and purging practices also have a significant role to play in enforcing the following FIPPs:

Data minimization

Despite extensive efforts to the contrary, information systems will often manage to collect and incorporate data beyond the scope of what is relevant or necessary. A robust method for flagging and ultimately purging data that is inadvertently stored or no longer useful helps protect personal and sensitive information from overexposure.

Use limitation

It's tempting to want to use data that was collected for one initial purpose to explore or fulfill some other, later identified analytical intention. However, this can infringe on the privacy standards accepted or consented to by data subjects. Implementing a thoughtful policy that imposes a strict retention regime will help avoid these temptations. Adhering to set conditions, such as an initially agreed upon time period (e.g., one year, data subject reaches age of majority, etc.), or some other clearly defined purge parameter (e.g., data subject leaves the care of Facility X) can aid in keeping data usage firmly grounded within the scope of its initial collection.

Security

As long as data persists, so too do the risks of loss, unauthorized access or use, modification, and unintended or inappropriate disclosure—no matter how secure the system or how exhaustively it controls access to and revelation of data. For information that has outlived its initially intended purposes, indefinite retention creates significant liabilities and risks. These can be minimized or avoided altogether by regularly purging the data.

Designing Deletes

Purge regimes can be carried out in an automated fashion, through manual intervention, or by using various hybrid methodologies. Different purging techniques will require different processes and implementations. Some can be automated to run on regularly scheduled jobs, while others always require manual attention from an administrator. No matter the design, you will need a way to identify all the relevant records, whether centralized in one directory or distributed across multiple databases.

To determine an adequate purge regime, it's important to *know the applicable policy and legal obligations*. If data-management retention practices are sound and data is well curated with lineage metadata (along the lines outlined above), it's much easier to establish more sophisticated purge processes. For example, automated notifications generated by the system as data-retention dates approach may be used to trigger analyst reviews to manually purge, extend retention dates, trigger additional reviews, change the data classification, or prescribe some other action or intervention.

The scheduling of purging events may depend significantly on the type of purging used. Nondeletion purging can typically be carried out while the system is online and in use. Deletion-purging techniques, however, may require that users are not working on the system or that it be taken down entirely. For example, with many common relational database types, reclaiming table rows marked for deletion will require that the table space be temporarily locked to avoid potential conflicts that might arise while concurrently writing to that table. In such cases, shutting down or freezing the database will be procedurally necessary to enact these backend deletion operations.

Finally, policy requirements or other considerations may dictate specific terms of reporting requirements for the purging event. For example, audit trails that capture purging events may, in so doing, preserve unwanted traces of records intended to be purged altogether. The question would then need to turn to whether to extend the notion of purging to the audit trails themselves or to otherwise minimize the details of the purge event capture in those audit trails.

Conclusion

The purging methods and implementation measures addressed in this chapter provide a breadth of options and important considerations for putting sensitive data out of reach. Both deletion and nondeletion purging practices include an array of techniques that achieve varying degrees of data irretrievability. Whether you intend to comply with relevant data-protection laws seeking to safeguard sensitive data from abuse, impose retention rules to reduce costs, maximize efficiencies, or ensure data quality, these approaches cover a wide assortment of potential use cases.

Letting go can be hard. But among the many lessons and facets of privacy engineering captured in this book, it is perhaps one of the most important for systems architects to embrace. Sometimes the most responsible approach to data stewardship is actually some principled form of letting it go.

PART IV

Putting It All Together

The building blocks of privacy are in your hands. Now it's time for you to figure out how to put them together. In Chapter 11, we walk through some hypothetical technologies and discuss how we might fashion a privacy-protective architecture using the capabilities described in this book. Meanwhile, if you're convinced of the importance of engineering privacy into your technology and want to make sure it develops as a core part of your organization, we offer a quick outline of how to find (or cultivate) your own Privacy Engineer in Chapter 12. Finally, in Chapter 13, we look to the future and just a few of the many privacy-related questions that the privacy-minded engineer might be called upon to answer.

CHAPTER 11

Practical Applications and Use Cases

Over the course of the preceding pages, we have described the foundational components of a privacy-protective information management architecture. Just like a set of building blocks, these capabilities can be combined in a wide variety of ways to create the final product. In some cases, you will find that you end up using more of one kind of block than another, and in others you might not use one particular block at all. In still other cases, you might need to design and build a bespoke privacy-enhancing technology as yet undreamt of and tailored to some set of unique circumstances. There are no absolute "right" answers when it comes to privacy: the ultimate design of your product will depend on the specific desires of you and your customers.

It may be helpful to see how our various building blocks interact. The following examples are not based on any particular real-world models, and the solutions we suggest are by no means the only possible privacy-protective configuration for the systems in these contexts. Indeed, you might be able to come up with far better configurations than we have. The intent is not to provide a guide to building these types of systems, but rather to demonstrate how some of the capabilities that have been described in the preceding chapters can fit together.

Basic Framework

Now that you're equipped with the ideas and techniques from the preceding chapters, let's return to the questions that were set out in "Before You Get Started" on page 17. Although this framework is by no means the only approach to thinking through privacy issues with a technology, it's one way to organize your approach to identifying and addressing privacy questions. As a refresher:

- Does this technology interact with personally identified or identifiable information?

- What is the technology supposed to do with the data?

- What *could* the technology do with the data?

- What are the potential privacy concerns?

- How can you configure your privacy building blocks to address those issues?

This guide will help you when you start to design your product, and you should repeat the process any time you add a new data set or create new functionality.

Use Case #1: Social Media Analysis

Social media platforms offer a trove of information about individuals, and much of that information is freely available to anyone with access to the Internet. Everyone from marketers to academic institutions to law enforcement and intelligence agencies wants to figure out how to derive valuable insight from those platforms. Can this be done in a way that preserves individual privacy? In this use case, we consider a hypothetical social media analysis product.

The technology
> You have designed a technology that analyzes social media information. Your product scrapes publicly available social media data, stores that data, and allows users to analyze this data in a variety of ways.[1]

Does this technology interact with personally identified or identifiable information?
> Yes. Social media information can contain personally identifiable information, including names, addresses, and telephone numbers. In addition, social media information might be highly identifiable. Geolocation information, statements regarding attendance at certain events, statements describing unique features of home, family, or social life, and other information might allow others to identify the individual even when they are not directly identified by PII.

> Social media information can also contain a substantial amount of other sensitive information about individuals, including religious affiliation, political opinion, health information, and sexual orientation. This information can be explicit (e.g., a statement that "I am a Catholic") or it can be inferred from other information in the data (e.g., weekly Sunday geolocation check-ins at a Catholic church).

---

1 Be aware that a website's Terms of Service may restrict the scraping of this type of data without permission from the website owners, and violation of those Terms of Service may expose you and/or your customers to criminal and civil liability. Be sure to read the Terms of Service and obtain consent where required. This is one of those situations where you absolutely should check with a lawyer before investing too much time and money in your product.

What is the technology supposed to do with the data?

Let's assume that your social media analysis technology is designed to scrape data from social media based on product mentions to allow corporate users to gain a better understanding of those users and their influence (possibly in order to engage with those users on some level to help promote the product). For example, the technology might search through social media platforms for all mentions of Brand X soda products and collect those mentions (in status updates, user profiles, etc.) as well as other public information about those users (demographic information, social network, etc.). The Brand X manufacturer can then analyze that data in order to understand the appeal of their product, gauge the effect of their advertising strategies, and evaluate the utility of social media as an advertising vehicle.[2]

What could *the technology do with the data?*

The technology will be working with significant amounts of unstructured data in the form of status updates, free-form profiles, and other such information, depending on the nature of the platform. Consequently, the technology will very likely collect more information than just that relevant to soda consumption. For example, references to Brand X might be included with a laundry list of other "Favorite Things" in a user profile. Alternatively, Brand X might be referenced in a context irrelevant to soda preference (e.g., "We were drinking Brand X that night when…"). Included in this over-collection of data could be sensitive information that most social media users would not expect (or condone) a private company with which the user has no pre-existing relationship to hold.

For social media platforms that do not require users to identify themselves but instead allow them to use pseudonymous handles, it may nonetheless be possible to identify individuals based on the aggregation of data points within the profile and posts on the platform (or even by comparing information on the platform with identified activities on other platforms or even outside the digital world). In addition, sophisticated data analytics could potentially expose other, nonobvious information about social media users based on the data collected, such as sexual orientation and religion (based on social network connections)[3] or even health

---

2 Not all social media scraping tools have to be used for corporate benefit. Another use could be for public health insights, such as conducting social media monitoring, along with computational linguistics and machine learning, to identify early warning signs of a possible epidemic by tracking references to particular diseases or symptoms, and reasoning where the people who mentioned them are located. Such insight could be extremely useful to society at large but still unnerving to individuals.

3 Carter Jernigan and Behram F.T. Mistree, "Gaydar: Facebook Friendships Expose Sexual Orientation" (*http://bit.ly/fm-gaydar*). *First Monday*, October 5, 2009.

conditions such as pregnancy.[4] These types of discoveries could strike many of the people located by such an analysis as disconcerting.

Also note the possibility of unsanctioned use of the data by analysts and other individuals with access to your technology. Any of the above analysis could be directed against individuals with a connection to the analyst and used to steal an identity or track the person with the intent to harass or cause physical harm.

What are the potential privacy concerns?

Each function or potential function above can raise privacy concerns, including the following:

- *Identify when a product is mentioned on a social media platform*: Although social media users should be aware that information not protected by privacy controls is public, they may nonetheless not intend for extensive personal information about them to be collected and maintained by third parties.

- *Identify the "influencers"—those whose comments reach the widest audience of social media consumers*: Even when social media users call attention to themselves by explicitly tagging a consumer product manufacturer or distributor, the collection of information regarding their social networks involves the collection of information on individuals who have no wish for the entity to collect and maintain information about them. They may even be completely unaware that someone in their social network mentioned the consumer product and therefore may have exposed them to such collection and analysis.

- *Identify anonymous users based on particular data in the collected information*: Users who wished to remain anonymous may find those preferences thwarted by data analytics those users do not even know exist. Identification of those users could have severe consequences for those individuals, especially if they rely on their anonymity for some purpose, such as avoiding political persecution.

- *Derive nonobvious information about social media users*: Users of social media who do not protect their activity through privacy controls presumably make a conscious choice to share this information with some audience. Derivation of nonobvious information may thwart user intent by revealing information about them that they have not knowingly shared (and may not ever have intended to make public).

---

4 Duhigg, Charles. "How Companies Learn Your Secrets" (*http://bit.ly/nyt-how-companies*). The New York Times. February 18, 2012.

- *Tracking and analysis of individuals for unsanctioned purposes (harassment, stalking, etc.)*: This one should be self-explanatory. Any unwanted attention experienced by an individual infringes on their right to privacy.

How can you configure your building blocks to address those issues?
Each privacy concern requires separate consideration:

- *Personal data collected without users' consent*: Obtaining individual consent for the use of the data would be advisable—and indeed is a core tenet of the FIPPs. Conditional access controls could be configured to only provide analysts access to the data if there is a record of consent in the system (or, if there is an indication of consent in the data itself, such as the tagging of Brand X in the social media activity).[5]

- *Collecting additional, nonuser personal information*: Adoption of granular, cell-level security controls would allow data stewards to remove identifying information from the social media data while still reaping analytic benefits from the data collected. Granular data management could also allow for the removal of any information from the data not directly relevant to the analysts' interests.

- *Piercing anonymity*: The identification of deidentified data generally requires analysis to be run against additional data sets to those containing the anonymous data. Put another way, in order to determine identity, you must compare your data to a data set with some identifying information. Functional access controls could be used to limit (or prevent altogether) the export of data in an electronic form that can then be processed against an identified data set.

- *Derivation of unintentionally disclosed information*: Such derivations can be produced in a variety of ways depending on the data in question, so there may be a variety of potential solutions. In general, the best strategy is to prevent the aggregation of the data necessary to arrive at these conclusions. Table-level access controls or federated system architecture can be used to keep potentially revelatory data sets apart. Temporal access controls might also limit the number of available data points available to drive accurate mosaic analysis.

---

5 Social media platforms would argue that they obtain valid consent for broad data usage from users who consent to their Terms of Service when signing up for the platform. There is an ongoing debate as to whether such consent should be considered sufficient—a debate we will refrain from entering into here. The alternative—obtaining valid, informed consent from individuals at scale—would be a significant and costly logistical challenge. But as with all such technical challenges, perhaps it only awaits the right innovator to devise a solution.

- *Misuse of data*: Audit logs should be configured to provide enough information to ensure accountability for anyone attempting to use the system to intentionally violate an individuals' privacy.

Use Case #2: Secure Messaging

Communications that are secure from eavesdropping, copying by a provider, or legal intercept (a fancy term for government wiretapping) have value to certain consumers. In this use case, we consider a hypothetical secure messaging application.

The technology

You're building a secure messaging service that allows users to exchange messages (not unlike email—but without all the legacy compatibility requirements). Users will interact with the messaging service either through a smartphone app or by using a traditional web application to securely exchange messages in a manner that is resistant to any sort of eavesdropping by virtue of sophisticated cryptography as it travels through the service.

Does this technology interact with personally identified or identifiable information?

Yes, absolutely. The service directly interacts with personal identifiable addresses that correspond to each user as well as the message traffic itself. In addition, the service will necessarily have access to the metadata (things like their IP address, pattern of recipients, time and frequency of messaging), which contain information about how those messages arrive to and are delivered through the messaging services infrastructure.

What is the technology supposed to do with data?

Usually, a system with privacy controls aims to strategically equip its users with limited access to data about other people. The privacy *adversary* is the users of the system. But in this case, that model is flipped, with the system itself being considered the adversary. First, your product must ensure that the contents of the messages are protected from the service itself, not to mention any entity that could compromise the service through technical (hacking) or legal (warrant, subpoena, or seizure by a government entity) means. Second, the service must minimize the privacy risk incurred by the metadata to the greatest extent possible while still operating the service. Here, risk can be mitigated by a careful collection and minimization strategy. Metadata necessary to operate the service will be collected and held as briefly as possible.

What could the technology do with the data?

If the security aspects of this system fail and data could actually be accessed by unauthorized parties, then it could become a durable archive of all the message traffic in the system as well as the metadata about when and where the messages originated from—essentially, exactly the same as the traditional email services that users explicitly sought to avoid. By looking at the contents of the message traffic, it could be used to deliver targeted ads. It could also enable re-identification of the individuals using the system, even when they have provided no personal identifiers in the creation of their accounts. Re-identification and location tracking can also occur through metadata, without access to message content. Even if users sign up to the service using pseudonyms, metadata can all be used to re-identify them in the dataset when correlated with other datasets where they are already identified. Finally, in a breach of the system, the sensitive information in the message content could be publicly released or privately stolen for nefarious purposes.

What are the potential privacy concerns?

Various privacy concerns are connected to different parts of the system, and should be mitigated separately. These concerns include:

- *Loss of confidentially of the message contents*: This risk applies to any user of the system once someone else (ranging from the service operator, to a law enforcement official, to a cyber attacker), gains access to the contents of a message via the services' infrastructure.

- *Re-identification using message contents*: Aside from leaking the potentially sensitive information in the messages themselves, the message contents could be used in re-identification. Combining specific details revealed in messages with other sources could identify the entities involved in any given message exchange.

- *Re-identification using metadata*: A combination of timestamps and IP address information can be used to uniquely identify individuals sending messages by cross-referencing or inference using other data sets like ISP logs or social network analysis.[6]

How can you configure your building blocks to address those issues?

Let's look at how the privacy risks outlined can be addressed through architectural decisions:

- *Loss of confidentially of the message contents and re-identification using message contents*: To ensure that contents of the messages will not be compromised, we can apply encryption to the message traffic. Keeping the messages

---

6 We are referring specifically to the academic discipline of social network analysis (SNA), which studies communications graphs to glean inferences about identity, community structure, and status. A different method of re-identification using the metadata mentioned here is traffic analysis of log data and correlating timing of events, which need not look at a social graph.

safe from the service means never allowing an unencrypted message to cross the service infrastructure.

Using public-key cryptography, each instance of the client software will generate its own public and private key pair, and store the private key while publishing the public key via the secure messaging-service infrastructure or some other key distribution service (see Figure 11-1). Key exchange poses a significant problem, especially given the threat of government coercion to surrender keys.[7] Handling private keys is a delicate business. Today, some smartphones have specialized hardware for securely storing private keys that can simplify this task for native applications. In web browsers, there is no safe way to do secure cryptography in Javascript,[8] but there are browser plugins that can safely store secret keys and securely run cryptographic functions.

The benefit of using public and private keys is that the client code can fully encrypt the messages before giving them to service infrastructure. Each sent message will consist of the intact list of recipients and the encrypted message. By ensuring the message contents remain confidential, the first two privacy risks are mitigated.

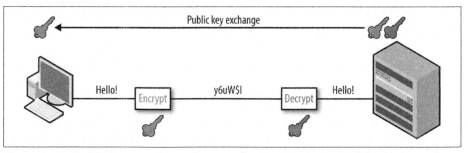

Figure 11-1. Public-key cryptography provides a common method for ensuring that message exchange occurs in a way such that an intercepted message cannot be read and that only the intended application services can make sense of the message content.

- *Re-identification using IP addresses*: This risk is harder to mitigate fully using technical means. All network traffic comes with an IP address associated with it. One of the simplest ways to re-identify someone is to link their IP address to their identity using the logs of the ISP or wireless carrier that is

---

7 For one novel approach to the difficult problem of key exchange, see the documentation of the CONIKS service (*http://bit.ly/coniks-docs*).

8 See "Javascript Cryptography Considered Harmful" (*http://bit.ly/js-cryptography*) for a full breakdown of why Javascript cryptography is not currently an option.

routing the address. The logs can be used to map the lease of the IP address to a specific customer. While it requires data not held by the service infrastructure, that information is not out of reach of a government.

To mitigate this risk, start by implementing a minimization or retention policy that limits the amount of time that IP address data is held. Such a policy could reasonably range from keeping a few days of logs (for troubleshooting and performance analytics purposes) to more stringent minimization that calls for IP addresses never to be recorded (other than transiently in the operation of the infrastructure). The amount of time an IP address is held is somewhat immaterial as long as it's reasonably short. However, this only limits privacy when studying the past. The service infrastructure can still be compelled to do logging of IP address data.

The only way to fully offset the privacy risk that an IP address represents is to never know the real IP address in the first place. The service could be designed to use a third-party VPN or proxy service, such that the service infrastructure never sees the true IP address of the clients. (Of course, your customers could choose to use such a service as well.) This will make it much more difficult to connect the use of the service to an identity-linked IP address. That said, while it may take more hops to trace IP back to its source, it's not impossible.

An example of a way to significantly defray the risks of re-identification via IP address is to run the secure messaging service on the Tor network. Tor supports the *hidden service protocol*, which offers substantial anonymity in IP communications between the clients and service.[9]

- *Re-identification using message metadata*: If a few nodes in a network of communications are compromised, it's possible to start identifying other nodes in the network by building inferences bases on the pattern, timing, and frequency of communications between various nodes in the network. In order to remove this particular risk, you can relax the notion of durable identifiers (even pseudonymous or randomized IDs) for each user in your network and instead use a technique called mailbox chaining to make it impossible to tie one act of communication to another.

Mailbox chaining requires that existing users are able to allocate new addresses using new credentials in an automatic fashion. As each message is

---

9 The developers of Tor (formerly TOR, the since-deprecated acronym for The Onion Router) acknowledge that, despite Tor's great strengths, there are still re-identification risks in certain specific circumstances, such as end-to-end traffic correlation if an ISP has records of the exact times users were online, or coarse-grained activity matching to correlate time periods of Tor use with time periods of activity occurrence that match multiple times. Nevertheless, Tor is often a good choice for protecting a user's location and defending against IP address metadata analysis.

composed, the client allocates a new mailbox. This new mailbox address is put into the encrypted message as the next-reply address—should the recipient wish to respond, the response is sent to this address. Since the link between the initial address and the next-reply address is established inside the encrypted message, the link can be considered secret. If each reply also comes from a new address, no two acts of communication can be easily linked via identifiers. The upshot here is that instead of a graph of communications that can be analyzed, the whole system just looks like messages exchanged between single-use addresses.

Use Case #3: Automated License Plate Readers (ALPR)

Law enforcement agencies are increasingly using automated recognition of license plates to assist in emergency and investigative workflows. The ability to capture license plate "reads" and associate them with the geo-temporal information of the time of the reading can help determine whether vehicles may have been involved in suspected criminal activity. The growing ubiquity of these mass surveillance tools has generated much concern in certain quarters. In this use case, we explore the hypothetical implementation of such a technology.

The technology

You're a technology administrator for your local police department and have received a federal grant to purchase automated license plate reader (ALPR) devices to deploy either on your department's vehicles or at fixed public locations throughout your municipality. You are also responsible for establishing a framework for utilizing the license plate reads captured by these devices. You're aware of the concerns raised by civil liberties advocacy groups, as well as questions raised by members of your own community in city council discussions. You've been directed to develop a plan to implement these capabilities in a way that is responsive to privacy concerns, but that also provides your law enforcement officers and analysts with the tools to fulfill their legitimate responsibility to public safety.

Does this technology interact with personally identified or identifiable information?

On the surface, ALPR data might appear to be a form of anonymized, nonidentifying information. The data captured by license plate readers is limited to images of license plates that are digitally processed to extract license plate alphanumeric characters, augmented with the capture event metadata (including geo-location, timestamps, and the type of device used for collection) and indexed for ease of recall. Though the license plate number itself is not directly personally identifying, the ability to somewhat readily link that plate with its owner (through vehicle registry or other data sources) may be construed in some jurisdictions as creating *effectively* personally identifying information.[10] Moreover, the images captured by these devices may, however rarely, inadvertently capture unequivocally identifying information, such as faces of drivers.

What is the technology supposed to do with data?

ALPR systems can assist law enforcement agencies by allowing them to identify and locate vehicles of interest during authorized investigative activity. Here, the primary privacy "adversary" is typically the ALPR user. A secondary "adversary" could be a potential unauthorized intruder who manages to gain access to the system. Providing safeguards to minimize over-collection, unwarranted use, repurposing, and unnecessary retention and dissemination of data, as well as critical security measures can protect privacy interests.

What could *the technology do with the data?*

In an unregulated environment, community members and privacy advocates may worry that the system could be used to support a ubiquitous surveillance regime for tracking the movements of innocent community members and suspected criminals alike. Concerns around law enforcement officers tracking protesters attending constitutionally protected political events or ex-spouses being tracked by the scorned have already generated media attention.[11] Detractors may assert that expansive collection of ALPR data undermines reasonable expectations of privacy in public spaces (i.e., on public roads) and that unfettered usage and indefinite retention offends proportionality principles. Furthermore, lack of understanding and accountability measures in place to oversee use of ALPR systems will likely only exacerbate these concerns and further undermine public trust in law enforcement agencies.

What are the potential privacy concerns?

The privacy concerns and community interests mentioned above should be treated discretely to begin to work toward appropriate mitigation strategies in designing such a system. Those concerns are:

- *Overly-broad collection of ALPR data*: ALPR units are unsophisticated in the sense that they operate by performing blanket image collection and processing based strictly on where they are located. They do not discriminate with

---

10 Ease of linking ALPR reads to vehicle registry information should not be universally assumed. Some jurisdictions place particularly firm restrictions on law enforcement agencies' abilities to access DMV records such as vehicle registries outside of specific procedural contexts that exclude many ALPR use cases. On the other hand, many law enforcement agencies *do* have access to DMV registries, and barring these kinds of jurisdictional restrictions, they can connect DMV records to ALPR reads without too much effort—and certainly far more easily than the general public.

11 Crump, Catherine. "Police Documents on License Plate Scanners Reveal Mass Tracking" (*http://bit.ly/aclu-mass-tracking*). American Civil Liberties Union. July 17, 2013.

regard to vehicle types and, unless they are turned on and off according to some prescribed collection regime, make no distinction between collecting plate reads for vehicles that may be the subject of suspicious activity or criminal investigation and reads for vehicles that have no suspect involvements. Proponents of ALPR systems argue that since these devices operate in public spaces, they are doing nothing more than taking photographs and processing images in the public sphere. Opponents argue that the volume and efficiency with which these devices operate makes them transcend manual image collection. Additionally, the ability to piece together a mosaic of such images across potentially expansive regions (limited only by the number and placement of these devices) creates novel concerns about reasonable expectations of privacy in the public domain.

- *Misidentification of license plates*: ALPR reader units rely on optical character recognition (OCR) to translate images of license plates into text that can then be indexed and searched. While OCR technology may have advanced to the point of providing a reasonably high rate of translation fidelity, errors still occur in cases of unfamiliar or out-of-state plates, inclement weather conditions, obfuscation of characters, and other situations. Such erroneous reads can cause vehicles (and their drivers) that have no connection to a law enforcement investigation to be inadvertently implicated in criminal activity.[12]

- *Re-identification of ALPR data*: Though ALPR data and license plates may not be directly personally identifying, the format and structure of the data may be such that linking the ALPR data through other information and analysis systems could make personal identification little more than a trivial step beyond the initial data collection event.

- *Abuse of ALPR data for unauthorized and illegal applications*: Advocacy groups may concede to the value of using ALPR reads in the investigation of vehicles that are suspected of involvement in active criminal cases. However, they might worry that departments will allow scope creep to present new uses of the data that have not been formerly authorized. The data could also be misused by bad actors within departments for tracking vehicles with no legitimate justification for inquiry (e.g., the jealous officer tracking the ex-spouse).

- *Indefinite retention of ALPR data exacerbating other privacy concerns over time*: The compounding storage of historical ALPR data may raise concerns

---

12 See Green v. California (*http://bit.ly/green-v-ca*) for an example of a law enforcement vehicular stop in which the misidentification of a single character in a license plate led to the plaintiff's vehicle being falsely identified and the plaintiff held at gunpoint.

that data collected without any initial suspicion of criminal involvement is applied many months later to investigations or character assessments that could not have been warranted at the time of initial collection. The ability to potentially construct patterns of life of community members may also raise fears of a repressive surveillance state that may have a chilling effect on constitutionally protected activities, such as free assembly.

How can you configure your building blocks to address those issues?

Let's explore these risks individually and evaluate design considerations that might be applied to help address each concern:

- *Overly-broad collection of ALPR data*: The collection concern is difficult to fully resolve. While protocols might be placed to prohibit the placement of ALPR cameras on private properties or near sensitive institutions and locations, data is still likely to be collected that implicates an overwhelming majority of vehicles that may never have any connection to a legitimate law enforcement investigation. If, at a policy level, administrators are willing to accept that extraneous ALPR reads are going to be unavoidably captured, the most important privacy mitigations will need to be addressed by analysis and retention practices.

- *Misidentification of license plates*: ALPR misidentification instances can be reduced or avoided altogether rather easily. Officers who need ALPR information must compare the alphanumeric readout to the image from which the license-plate characters were derived and ensure a proper match. Simple system design choices, such as creating dynamic icons that incorporate the ALPR image for each record and display them prominently alongside the OCR-derived license plate text, can ensure the visual inspection process does not needlessly impede investigative workflows.

- *Re-identification of ALPR data*: The ability to readily associate other identifying vehicle records (e.g., vehicle registry information) with ALPR data may motivate additional authorizations at the point of drawing in re-identifying data. The ALPR analysis capability may therefore be configured in such a way that allows analysts or users to search for raw license plate numbers, but in order to further associate numbers of interest with identifying records, analysts may need to document or certify some motivating level of suspicion, a case number, or other formalized authorization.

- *Abuse of ALPR data for unauthorized and illegal applications*: Controlling for unauthorized and illegal applications of ALPR data is an exemplary reason for using purpose- and/or scope-driven revelation practices. By codifying specific purposes for use of ALPR data, queries against the system can be configured such that users must submit an authorized search purpose. The purpose entered may then be used to further limit the set of results according to geo-spatial or temporal constraints associated with each permitted purpose.

While purpose-driven data revelation may be required to run a search query, it doesn't explicitly prevent a nefarious user from falsely entering a search purpose in order to return desired results that may not be authorized for the investigation at hand. However, there's a good chance the affirmative purpose entry requirement will prompt the user to think twice about deception. Moreover, entering a false search purpose should be logged by the system's audit trails to ensure that subsequent administrative or supervisory inquiries have a reliable record to draw upon when holding the user accountable for malfeasance.

In environments where a history of ALPR records abuse warrants heightened and proactive scrutiny of user searches, the system can be configured to require per-query supervisor review and authorization process prior to returning the requested results. By introducing a layer of manual review that is bound to generate analysis latency, the system introduces a tradeoff between workflow efficiency and active oversight. This tradeoff may not be tolerable for agencies where timely results are mission critical. But it may provide a tolerable compromise for agencies that may otherwise be stripped of ALPR data access without a more aggressive review regime.

- *Indefinite retention of ALPR data exacerbating other privacy concerns over time*: In order to decide whether ALPR data should be retained and for how long, you should first examine the justifications for using that data. If, for example, your ALPR data collection is warranted strictly for running the license plate numbers against a known set of vehicles associated with previously identified crimes, you only need to keep the data for the time that it takes to complete those "hotlist" checks. Afterward, nonmatching ALPR reads can be purged.

On the other hand, if your department insists on the value of retaining historical ALPR data in order to inform potential future investigations, you may want to conduct an empirical analysis of investigations involving ALPR data to set sensible polices for retaining the data. If such an analysis reveals, for example, a sharp drop in the utility of ALPR data that is 18 months old or more, this can serve as a strong, data-driven justification to establish 18 months as the limit in an overarching retention policy. After 18 months, you then may choose to adopt an appropriate deletion method from among the options outlined in Chapter 10 and as required by policy and other practical considerations.

Conclusion

These examples should provide you with a rough idea for how to think about privacy in the context of designing and building a product. They aren't perfect; the various mitigations proposed in each use case do not necessarily completely address the potential privacy concerns we have described. In some cases, they must be supported by other, nontechnical actions in order to be effective. In other cases, there may not be any combination of technical and policy mitigations that resolve the privacy concerns to total satisfaction. In yet other cases, there may be some completely new and better technical or policy approach that the world (or at least this book) has yet to address. How you decide to proceed with your own product will very much depend on the wider context in which you are developing it—your business objectives, your profit margins, and the numerous other nonprivacy factors you have to weigh as you create your product.

CHAPTER 12

Enter the Privacy Engineer

Congratulations! If you've made it this far, you've hopefully designed and built a technology using some combination of the capabilities outlined in the previous chapters (and perhaps even a few innovations of your own). You slap a label on the box (actual or metaphorical), proudly declaring the technology to be "engineered for privacy." Now you can turn your attention to other exciting matters, such as getting people to use it, confident that you have done your part to make privacy safe in an uncertain world.

Sadly, this is highly unlikely. Privacy is not something that can be fully addressed with a few architectural decisions made in the design phase alone. A commitment to privacy is an ongoing one, and as your technology grows and is adopted by more and more users in a variety of contexts, you will need to devote organizational resources to maintaining your commitment. Consequently, a key component of maintaining your privacy architecture is going to be an individual (or individuals) responsible for just that.

This requires a Privacy Engineer.

The Role of the Privacy Engineer

The concept of a Privacy Engineer is still very much in its infancy, so it may very well mean different things to different people. We define it broadly as the person (or persons) at your company responsible for ensuring your product is developed, built, and used in a manner consistent with your company's privacy values. In short, if you have a vision for how your product is going to shape the world when it comes to individual privacy, then your Privacy Engineer (and her team) will be helping you implement that vision.

An effective Privacy Engineer is going to be integral to a significant portion of your organization's activities. So, what does she do all day?

Product design

Privacy should be under discussion by your design team from as close to day one as possible. Once you have identified a concept and determined that the execution of your technology is going to require some interaction with personally identifiable information, then a Privacy Engineer should be at the whiteboard with the rest of your team, pitching privacy-protective designs into the mix as your technology takes shape. The Privacy Engineer should then maintain an ongoing close relationship with the design team, contributing to the continuing evolution of the technology throughout its lifespan.

Distribution strategy

How should you distribute your technology? If it's a commercial product, to whom should you sell it? What distribution channels should you enter next? What new capabilities should you develop for your technology? The answers to these and other critical strategic questions should take privacy issues into consideration. Certain customers may be more or less open to using your technology based on privacy considerations. Legal regimes in some countries might make it difficult (or impossible) to use certain technologies. Evolving law, policy, or perceptions of privacy might suggest that certain designs are more advantageous than others (and may even create a competitive advantage for you over others in your sector). While your Privacy Engineer's input may not often be the deciding factor in developing your distribution strategy, it can provide essential information that will lead to smarter decision-making.

Customer support

Until the magical day when every company has a Privacy Engineer, your Privacy Engineer will likely also be your *customers'* Privacy Engineer. Having been intimately involved in every aspect of the design and having carefully thought through the assorted privacy imperatives affecting likely users of the technology, a Privacy Engineer can provide critical support to customers trying to use it in a privacy-protective manner. Ideally, your Privacy Engineer will function as a consultant, suggesting alternative ways to use the capabilities described throughout this book to enable the efficient operation of your technology while meeting assorted privacy requirements. Consequently, this will help your users use the product more effectively, and sidestep potential legal violations or public controversy that otherwise might cripple your relationship with the customer and prevent them from further investment in your technology.

Marketing/user adoption

In an increasingly privacy-sensitive market, you will want to promote your privacy-enhancing features as a value-add for your technology. If you have invested the time and energy to design and build a privacy-protective technology, then you should make the promotion of those features a key part of your outreach to potential users. Your Privacy Engineer will know the key words and phrases that catch the eye of the privacy community and the public at large to help them identify products that address their privacy concerns. Your Privacy Engineer will also be able to identify clumsy phrasing that might unnecessarily spark privacy concerns that could undermine your promotion efforts.

Public relations privacy missteps can cause companies significant headaches. For example:

- Following the infamous "wardrobe malfunction" suffered by Janet Jackson during her Super Bowl XXXVIII half-time performance, digital video recording provider Tivo released statistics declaring the incident to be the most watched moment to-date on its device, surprising many customers who may not have been fully aware that their own activities were so closely tracked by the service provider.[1]

- Uber, a transportation service provider that is accessed via individual smartphones, sparked controversy when it published analyses of its customers' usage habits that indicated when they were likely engaging in "one-night stands."[2]

- In 2010, Microsoft Executive Dennis Durkin suggested that images collected via the camera included in their Kinect gaming interface might be used to support targeted advertising to users. The company quickly denied any possibility that the technology would be used in this way.[3]

These and other similar incidents could be avoided by having a Privacy Engineer as a core component of any PR communications team.

Lobbying

Privacy Engineers should also work with your government lobbying team to ensure privacy messaging is a part of their outreach. While privacy is sometimes not the highest priority issue for many policymakers, there are still a number of them who (thankfully) invest time and energy into engaging in privacy questions. Anticipating this interest when you know your technology raises privacy

---

1 Charny, Ben. "TiVo Watchers Uneasy after Post-Super Bowl Reports" (*http://bit.ly/tivo-janet*). CNET. February 5, 2004.

2 Pagliery, Jose. "Uber Removes Racy Blog Posts on Prostitution, One-night Stands" (*http://bit.ly/cnn-uber-data*). CNNMoney. November 25, 2014.

3 Gallagher, Dan. "Is Your Videogame Machine Watching You?" (*http://bit.ly/wsj-durkin*). Digits. November 11, 2010.

concerns can help avoid a negative first impression that can be hard to correct (especially when dealing with busy policymakers with limited spare attention).

Additionally, you may need to lobby policymakers directly on privacy-focused statutes and regulations that could affect your product. You might also want to participate in ongoing legal cases (via legal action on your own behalf or through amicus briefs) whose outcomes could affect the privacy landscape in which you operate. This will require your Privacy Engineer to stay up-to-date on current events and the latest thinking in privacy theory in order to anticipate changes and engage in these ongoing discussions where necessary. This role is also not exclusive to self-interested advocacy. There is a dearth of technical knowledge in the policymaking community, and if your organization and your Privacy Engineer are playing an active role in the privacy world by providing expert technical advice, then not only are you enhancing your company's reputation as smart on privacy but you are also making an overall positive contribution to society.

Other communications

In addition to policymakers, your Privacy Engineer should also be part of an effort to forge relationships with academia and the advocacy community. Many people in both areas are very interested in active engagement on privacy issues and are open to proactive outreach that begins a broader discussion around privacy. An open and frank dialogue can both reassure academics and advocates that your technology is privacy-friendly, and might even generate useful suggestions from these experts on ways to improve your technology and overall offering.

In some cases, academics and advocates may still ultimately determine that the privacy-utility cost-benefit analysis does not favor your technology and criticize it (and possibly lobby for regulations against its use). Nonetheless, your attempts at outreach are unlikely to be fruitless. First, by being transparent about what you are building and how it works, you can ensure that if there is criticism of your work then at least it's based on fact rather than poorly informed perceptions of what you do gleaned from third parties. Second, the personal relationships between your Privacy Engineer and your critics can temper the potential for rabid demagoguery that might otherwise characterize criticisms of your organization. It's much easier for critics to call a faceless corporate entity "evil" when they don't actually know anyone who works there.

Legal support

Your Privacy Engineer is not your lawyer, but she should have a close relationship with your legal team. Privacy requirements will frequently be incorporated into contracts and other operating agreements (often quasi-masked as "security" provisions). The Privacy Engineer—who will be familiar with privacy law and policy and how your technology can be used to implement those requirements—will be able to provide valuable input into the negotiation of these clauses.

In many cases, negotiations over these provisions will be occurring between your Privacy Engineer and non-technical lawyers working for those who want to use your technology. These lawyers will not have been a part of the sales pitches, the development of any statement of work, or even necessarily any of the internal discussions of how to use the product that is being purchased. Consequently, they will have—at best—a vague understanding of how the product in question works, and they will likely be pushing for broad, "cover-your-ass" provisions in their contracts that provide the maximum shield for legal liability with no appreciation for the actual workings of your technology. Your Privacy Engineer will be able to translate your technical speak for these lawyers and help to negotiate contract provisions that are in the best interests of both parties and that are reasonably tailored to the specifics of how your technology actually functions.[4]

In addition, if your organization deals with any personal data (hint: if you have personnel that work for you, it does), then you need your Privacy Engineer to play a role in the development and implementation of your own internal privacy policy. While at the end of the day such a policy regarding your own data may be totally unrelated to the privacy issues that may be implicated in your product, your organization's privacy policy is a visible representation of your overall commitment to privacy. Poor handling of personnel data, lack of adequate data security, a draconian and unnecessarily intrusive information security policy, and other internal privacy issues can undermine your image as a company that highly values privacy and has any expertise in the topic.

Employee education

Let's be realistic—in a growing organization, almost no department is overstaffed or even adequately staffed, and your top priority will likely not be staffing your Privacy Engineering team. As a result, your Privacy Engineer is going to be stretched thin and as your organization grows she is going to be sorely pressed to maintain full situational awareness of every privacy-relevant activity. In order to ensure that potentially critical privacy issues are identified and addressed across your organization, you are going to need to incorporate privacy into your personnel's core values so that they are sensitive to these issues and know when to seek out the Privacy Engineer. This requires extensive and ongoing education that your Privacy Engineer will need to develop and administer. New employee orientation will need to include a privacy component, and employees will need to

---

4 This is not to suggest that your Privacy Engineer should function in the place of your lawyer. Rather, she will support your lawyer in the fashioning of any legal agreement. Never negotiate an agreement—or anything, really—without a lawyer.

be kept up-to-date on the latest developments in privacy and why they are relevant to their work.

Privacy Engineers: How to Find One

You may have noticed that we've just described someone with the skills of an engineer, marketer, business strategist, lawyer, lobbyist, and philosopher, among other capabilities. It's a tall order. You are probably not simply going to be able to search LinkedIn for a list of "privacy engineers" and discover a convenient list of possible candidates (although with luck that will change in the very near future). In some cases, you may not even be able to find a single individual to fill the role—you might need to assemble a team of people that as a whole possesses the requisite skillset to effectively play this role.

Your perfect Privacy Engineer (and her team) will probably be built gradually as they work for you. Consequently, you want to look for a set of core competencies that will grow and develop along with a deep understanding of your technology, your organization's mission, and its privacy values. Those competencies, described in the following sections, should include at minimum:

- Strong domain expertise
- Ability to apply that expertise at a practical level
- Expert communications skills
- Solid engineering abilities
- Tempered passion

Domain expertise

The legal and policy basis of privacy is lengthy and complex. Privacy law and policy cannot be broken down into a short set of easy guidelines, and privacy issues can lurk in unexpected places. Depending on the context in which your technology will operate, a Privacy Engineer might need to understand privacy law as it relates to law enforcement, government intelligence collection, health care, insurance, financial institutions, consumer rights, employment law (including rules for employee unionization), education, etc. Or, it's possible your technology may generate an entirely new set of data or use data in a completely novel way, such that your Privacy Engineer needs to try to anticipate how privacy law might develop around this new case by analogizing it to any number of existing privacy laws (or more likely, some amalgamation of those laws).

Domain expertise encompasses more than just a broad understanding of the nuts and bolts of privacy law. Truly understanding privacy means understanding differing cultural perceptions of privacy as well, and if your organization is going to operate globally, then the Privacy Engineer will need to understand the law in these contexts in each country in which you are likely to operate. People in the United States value different aspects of privacy than people in France, Germany, or Japan. Knowledge of these distinctions is essential to being able to provide useful advice as to how to design and market privacy-implicating technology for government, business, or the general public in those countries. Different capabilities will be required to appropriately address different cultural imperatives, but identifying these imperatives will involve more than just understanding a laundry list of laws. Knowledge of historical context as well as privacy-related current events in countries that your business targets allows your Privacy Engineer to provide important advice regarding your operational environment.

Don't spend a ton of time looking for a privacy savant with an eidetic memory. You are unlikely to find a candidate who is going to have all of this law memorized along with experience in all of these fields. It will be enough for your Privacy Engineer to at least be able to recognize when these particular contexts will apply to your work. When given a use case for your technology, your Privacy Engineer should be able to identify the various legal regimes that might apply, and know how to research those regimes to learn more about how they may affect your product. In some cases, cursory research is not going to be enough, so you should also make sure you hire someone who knows their limits and will seek out advice from subject-area experts.

Practical application

While you want solid domain expertise in your Privacy Engineer, you don't want an academic. Privacy is a fascinating field and many people can wax philosophical about it at great length, but at the end of the day you are running an organization with a mission, not an 18th-century French salon. Once a Privacy Engineer identifies the law, policy, cultural, and other imperatives that might apply to your technology, she must then determine exactly what that means for your design, your regulatory obligations, your marketing, your government lobbying, your talent recruiting, and many other aspects of your business. In other words, you need someone who can take this domain expertise and translate it into practical advice for your organization.

As any quick survey of the general field of privacy will show you, this is not an easy skill to find. The great bulk of privacy expertise remains firmly ensconced in academia, where theoretical discussion is rich but application is thin. Academic works are a great place for someone to research and understand how the reasonable expectation of privacy standard for U.S. Fourth Amendment law has and will continue to develop, but few (if any) scholarly articles on the subject will provide a useful list of concrete technical features that should be a core component of, say, a social media analysis tool. Privacy advocates aren't necessarily the right fit, either. While they tend to be more focused on the actual details of implementing privacy law and theory, and will certainly be more familiar with the operations of government organizations or corporate entities than academics, more often than not they focus on engendering legal and policy solutions that address privacy issues at large, rather than developing particular technological tweaks for specific applications. All this is not to say that practical-minded academics or advocates don't exist. However, given the nature of those pursuits, there is simply less of a need for practical skills, and so those individuals tend to be less developed in this area.

The ideal Privacy Engineer will be someone who has experience actually *building* something that has had to operate according to some kind of parameters. Rather than seeing regulation as something that prohibits a particular technological innovation, she should see privacy-driven requirements for a particular capability as merely calling for additional features that address those requirements while still enabling the ultimate functionality. Consider the car. When engineers initially designed and built a car, they likely did not view the requirement that a car should be able to stop as something that hampered the design and therefore counseled against building a car at all. Just as braking is an essential component of any moving vehicle, so too should technical support for privacy protection be thought of as an essential component to any data-driven technology. A good Privacy Engineer will embrace this mentality.

Communication skills

By now you're well aware that privacy is a complicated topic, and likely agree that the details of engineering could hardly be classified as easy to understand without considerable training. A Privacy Engineer sits at the nexus of multiple fields and must often serve as a conduit between the engineers and the lawyers, regulators, and privacy-interested public. Consequently, strong communication skills are essential in an effective Privacy Engineer.

Our experience as Privacy Engineers has shown us that there is sometimes a basic incompatibility between the matter-of-fact, straightforward engineering mindset and the squirrelly, spiral-staircase lawyer (or philosopher) mindset. Engineers live in a binary world of ones and zeroes, or it works/it doesn't work dichotomies, and will often ask simply, "What is the *right* answer?" Lawyers and philosophers, trained to see an issue from all sides, are often loathe to (or, less charitably, are unable to) make such a stark declaration of the "right" solution, particularly with regard to the vaguely defined question of privacy. As a result, it's important for Privacy Engineers to be able to provide engineers (and others) not steeped in the intricacies of the privacy debate with enough information to be able to make an informed value judgment as to how their technology should address privacy concerns. They must be able to explain complex aspects of privacy law and policy in a concise, easy-to-understand way that helps engineers (and CEOs) decide on a specific course of action.

Engineering skills

As the title suggests, Privacy Engineering is more than just opining on legality, ethics, and media relations. Privacy Engineers are expected to actually contribute to the design and building of practical capabilities that meet privacy goals. An effective Privacy Engineer will need to be able to contribute to your design team at a technical level.

A policy expert who can write Java code or build SQL databases is difficult to find, but not impossible.[5] However, short of such an individual, a strong Privacy Engineer will at least show some ability to understand the "under the hood" mechanics of your product. This will lead to better-informed practical advice from your Privacy Engineer, who can thus tailor her practical guidance to better accommodate what is and is not actually possible within the technical confines of the system.

As your organization grows and you begin to reap the benefits of privacy-conscious design choices, you should consider devoting more engineering resources (i.e., skilled coders) specifically to your Privacy Engineering team. The more technically proficient your Privacy Engineering team, the more likely they can provide significant value to your ultimate technology design. Privacy Engineers who can actually write code and build technical capabilities not only can contribute to essential capabilities but they can also focus on directly building privacy-enhancing features that, while not necessarily at the top of a user's demand list, add significant value to the ultimate technology and may even contribute to your overall competitive advantage in a crowded marketplace.

Tempered passion

Privacy Engineering is a frustrating pursuit. Anyone who follows the ups and (mostly) downs of privacy in the modern age will know that when set against just about any other imperative, privacy loses. All too often, security trumps privacy, economic gain trumps privacy, and ease of use trumps privacy. When one benefit is often so clear and concrete and the other is so abstract, the abstract concept almost never prevails. This can even happen in the most privacy-conscious organization, where almost inevitably there will come a time when the desire to reach a mission-critical goal persuades decision-makers to opt for a course of action that falls short of what a privacy idealist would seek. Therefore, your Privacy Engineer needs to be able to handle losing a battle. A lot.

Maintaining zeal for the job requires a level of passion for privacy that remains undiminished in the face of the inevitable string of disappointments that a Privacy Engi-

---

5 Programs like the University of Colorado's Silicon Flatirons Center (*http://www.siliconflatirons.com*) are beginning to produce an increasing number of individuals with this combination of skills.

neer will face. Your Privacy Engineer needs to care so deeply about privacy that they can mount a passionate case for privacy against long odds and then lose that case with disappointing frequency. She must then be able to take that loss in stride while looking for constructive ways to contribute to the course of action ultimately taken by the organization. A good Privacy Engineer will care about privacy, but also not threaten to resign every time the tide does not go her way.

Avoiding Privacy Tunnel Vision

Let's say you now have a Privacy Engineer (or a few) working at your organization. They produce practical recommendations on how to address privacy issues in your technology. When you go to your Privacy Engineering team and ask for advice, they quickly and unanimously present you with a solution. This is great, right?

Wrong. Your Privacy Engineering team should be fighting with itself (politely, of course). Or, if you only have one Privacy Engineer, then you need to find someone able to challenge her. Privacy is difficult and nuanced, and if your Privacy Engineering team is offering you pat answers then you are probably missing vital perspectives that can only make your organization and your technology stronger. For example, does an employer have a right to monitor everything that its employees do using employer-provided equipment (computers, networks, email systems, etc.)? There is certainly no global consensus on this question, and as you develop your own internal policies and build technologies that might be used as part of an employee oversight program, you are going to want to hear all sides of the question. Consequently, you need a Privacy Engineer who can see and fairly present all sides of the issue or, more ideally, a couple of Privacy Engineers who will debate the issue and present you with differing perspectives to inform your decision.

You might also want to consider building a privacy-focused advisory board. This group should be composed of experts from varied backgrounds—academics, advocates, legal practitioners, former government officials, etc.—who can offer a variety of perspectives on difficult privacy questions that your organization may be facing. This group will be compensated, of course, but their primary livelihood will not depend on your company. This means they will be able to offer perspectives not colored by specific organizational interests. This "pure" privacy advice will be useful to you as you try to incorporate privacy into your broader decisions. This group can also be a good foil for your Privacy Engineers if they need additional voices to challenge their entrenched opinions.

Finally, your Privacy Engineers should take advantage of the many privacy-related events that take place around the world each year. These conferences gather experts on privacy from academia, advocacy, business, and government (both current and former officials), and they cover a myriad of privacy-related topics. From standard keynote speech-and-panel formats to more interactive paper workshops and problem-solving forums, these conferences present great opportunities for Privacy Engineers to keep up with current events and the latest trends in privacy theory as well as promoting (and getting feedback on) your own technical solutions to privacy challenges. In addition, the global privacy community is not particularly large, meaning that regular attendance at these conferences can be an excellent means of building important relationships with key players in the privacy field.

Selected Privacy Conferences

Amsterdam Privacy Conference (http://www.apc2015.net/)
> Hosted by the University of Amsterdam, this event occurs sporadically and gathers policymakers, technologists, advocates, and academics for in-depth privacy discussions in a variety of formats.

Computers, Privacy, and Data Protection (http://www.cpdpconferences.org)
> An international conference covering a wide variety of topics, primarily through panel discussions involving a mix of policymakers, technologists, advocates, and academics.

International Conference of Data Protection and Privacy Commissioners (http://bit.ly/art29-wp)
> This conference gathers government officials with responsibility for data protection and privacy for an annual closed meeting to discuss privacy issues. Some (but not all) conferences include privacy-related events that are open to the public. Follow the Article 29 Working Party for announcements of future events.

International Information Security and Privacy Conference (https://ifipsec.org/2015/)
> A technically focused conference bringing together diverse practitioners to discuss security and privacy.

Privacy Enhancing Technologies Symposium (https://petsymposium.org/2015/)
> A global gathering of privacy and anonymity experts to discuss advances in pro-privacy technologies.

Privacy Law Scholars Conference[6]
> Authors present scholarly papers pre-publication for review and discussion by leading privacy minds.

Symposium on Usable Privacy and Security (SOUPS) (http://bit.ly/soups-2015)
> An interdisciplinary conference focusing on human-computer interaction, security, and privacy.

---

6 *Alternates between Berkeley and George Washington University. Search "privacy law scholars conference" for information about the latest conference.*

Conclusion

Privacy Engineers are an essential component for any organization that wants to succeed in building and selling a privacy-conscious technology. The combination of knowledge and skills necessary for a good Privacy Engineer is rare, meaning you will have to work hard to find and keep a skilled engineer. Nevertheless, you should make the effort, as your Privacy Engineers can provide a significant value-add for your organization and constitute a key factor in your ultimate success or failure.

CHAPTER 13

The Future of Privacy

The development of technology has outpaced the development of the law. Nothing suggests that this will change in years to come. New technologies will be introduced to the market and often be widely adopted long before their potential privacy implications are even appreciated, let alone controlled for through law, policy, or other means. Consequently, it's hard to gaze into a crystal ball and extract some coherent vision of the future of privacy and technology.

Nonetheless, it's important that we try. Legal and regulatory changes can often have significant consequences for technology, including potentially requiring such major changes to the operation of a product that it's no longer a viable business proposition. In some cases, just the changing societal conceptions of privacy values may drive consumers away from your product if it's perceived as not privacy-protective enough (even though it might still be within the requirements of the law). Designing a product that anticipates these potential developments by having a flexible privacy architecture that can adapt with relative ease will prove a significant edge in a competitive technology marketplace.

But how might law and technology change in the next few years, and what can you do to keep up with it?

The "Death" of Privacy

Privacy itself is frequently declared dead, prompting those of us in the privacy field to trot out some version of Mark Twain's timeless rejoinder to erroneous reports of his own death:

- "Unfortunately, online anonymity is dead." —Ladar Levison, founder of LavaBit, an email service that Levison shut down in the wake of revelations of U.S. government surveillance.[1]

- "Privacy as we knew it in the past is no longer feasible…. How we conventionally think of privacy is dead." —Margo Seltzer, Harvard computer science professor speaking at the World Economic Forum in Davos in January 2015.[2]

- "I think we've clearly reached a point in today's world where privacy is pretty much a lost cause. Our information is already out there and regardless of how hard we scream that we want it back or want it to be secure, it's not going to happen…ever." —Jacob Morgan, author, in a 2014 column for *Forbes* magazine.[3]

- "You have zero privacy anyway. Get over it." —Scott McNealy, Sun Microsystems CEO, way back in 1999.[4]

However, in spite of these lurid declarations of the dramatic demise of privacy, the fact remains that as long as there are blinds on windows, privacy in some form will exist. But just what form it will take in the next decade is far from certain. The concept of privacy as currently conceived is not steeped in a particularly long history, and although that concept may not necessarily die, it might take a future form that is unrecognizable when compared to today's understanding.

Before the advent of easy travel and big cities, people lived their whole lives in small towns. Anyone who has ever lived in a small town can attest to the fact that everyone often knows everyone else's business. But with the expansion of the U.S. following the Civil War—resulting in both more places to go in the rural West and larger cities in the East—it became more readily possible to lose oneself in the crowd.[5] If modern technology now makes those changes meaningless by creating virtual worlds of information without walls and interconnecting the planet so completely that you can never disappear into obscurity, then have we in fact returned to the natural state of the world as it existed before a brief century (or so) of privacy that has now come and gone?

All this is not to suggest that one outcome is necessarily better but rather to point out that privacy is by no means a done deal. Historically, it's susceptible to changing soci-

---

1 Pagliery, Jose. "Online Privacy Is Dead" (*http://bit.ly/cnn-privacy-dead*). CNNMoney. October 17, 2013.

2 Carter, Richard. "Privacy Is Dead, Harvard Professors Tell Davos Forum" (*http://bit.ly/yahoo-privacy-dead*). Yahoo! Tech. January 22, 2015.

3 Morgan, Jacob. "Privacy Is Completely And Utterly Dead, And We Killed It" (*http://bit.ly/forbes-privacy-dead*). *Forbes*. August 19, 2014.

4 Sprenger, Polly. "Sun on Privacy: Get Over It" (*http://bit.ly/wired-privacy*). *Wired*. January 26, 1999.

5 Shank, Russell. "Privacy: History, Legal, Social, and Ethical Aspects" (*http://bit.ly/shank-privacy*). *Library Trends* 35, no. 1 (1986): 11.

etal values based on a re-evaluation of the benefits of privacy weighed against the potential societal benefits of greater transparency into individual lives and homes. Securing health information in the interests of preserving an individual's dignity and offering protection from potential stigmatization is a valid interest, but you could also make a case that greater transparency of healthcare information could be used to improve medical treatments for all patients and more effectively halt the spread of communicable diseases.[6] In some future world ravaged by more virulent disease, the interests of better healthcare and preventing the spread of illness might be found to outweigh individual privacy preferences, and the law and policy that now vigorously protect health information as particularly sensitive might change accordingly.

But changes in the conception of privacy may not be as simple as a re-evaluation of whether there should be more or less information disclosed in particular contexts. Changes might be subtler and far more complex. For example, imagine a society in which technology continues to drive ever-more data exposure and that makes it nearly impossible for even privacy-minded people to totally control the revelation of personal information. This society might develop a set of norms in which even though certain pieces of sensitive information are known about individuals, it's never acknowledged or used by those it does not concern.[7] This society of effectively willful blindness would require a complete rethinking of how the architecture described in this book might be applied (if it can be at all) to this new privacy paradigm.

While blanket declarations of privacy's death and burial might fall more on the side of hype and sensationalism than accuracy and nuance, if past is prologue, privacy as we know it could readily be unrecognizable to the next generation.

Legal Reform

Law and policy development lags significantly behind technological evolution, but it's not standing still. The next 10 years (or even just the next five) could see significant changes to the global privacy legal regime.

The first place to look for inspiration may be Europe. While the Fair Information Practice Principles may have been created in a U.S. government report (as you may recall from Chapter 1), the E.U. has long since taken the lead on the development of information privacy (i.e., data protection) policy. In 1995, the E.U. Parliament adop-

---

6 Ozimek, Adam. "The Future Of Healthcare Is Less Privacy." (*http://bit.ly/healthcare-privacy*) *Forbes.* June 27, 2014.

7 We see shades of this in the "as-if" tradition still influential in Japan today. "The as-if tradition requires that information overheard but not explicitly given is treated as if one did not have it. This allowed, for example, spouses to have arguments without the rest of the household treating them as though their marriage was in trouble, unless one or both partners approached a third party for help or advice in the matter." The Japanese Sense of Information Privacy (*http://bit.ly/adams-japan*), A.A. Adams, et al., p. 4.

ted its Data Protection Directive requiring E.U. member states to enact and enforce basic data-protection requirements for the use of personal information by both public and private sector organizations (although due to jurisdictional tensions between member states and the E.U., the requirements for nongovernmental organizations are somewhat more rigorous).[8]

The E.U. data protection model quickly became a global standard, in part because it required that organizations could only share data with other organizations in countries with what the E.U. considered an adequate level of data protection. Consequently, many countries hoping to do business with Europe adopted data-protection regimes similar to the European regime. Those that did not—such as the U.S., which the E.U. determined did not offer an adequate level of data protection within its borders—were forced to reach separate accommodations if they wanted to do any business that required the collection, use, or sharing of data about European citizens.[9] As such, if a private-sector entity is operating in one of these countries today, then it's more than likely following European data-protection rules.

In 2012, the E.U. began the process of strengthening and expanding its data-protection regime with the introduction of a new General Data Protection Regulation (*http://bit.ly/eu-data-protect*). The proposed regulation contains a number of provisions that represent significant and potentially far-reaching changes in privacy law, including:

- A broader jurisdictional reach for E.U. data-protection requirements
- The adoption of a "right to be forgotten" under which individuals can demand that organizations delete data about them when there are no legitimate grounds for retaining it
- A requirement (*http://europa.eu/rapid/press-release_IP-12-46_en.htm?locale=en*) that consent by the data subject be more explicitly given for data-processing activities

While the ultimate prospects of this proposal remain subject to the vagaries of the labyrinthine E.U. lawmaking process, the passage of some new data-protection legislation at some point in the next few years seems all but certain. The implementation of this new law will take some time of course, and other countries will again have to consider adapting to meet the new European model (and that process will itself depend on the internal politics within those countries). Nevertheless, if Europe con-

---

8 European Parliament and Council Directive 95/46/EC of October 25, 1995 on the protection of individuals with regard to the processing of personal data and on the free movement of such data (*http://bit.ly/eu-personal-data*). (Official Journal L 281 of 23.11.1995).

9 U.S.-E.U. Safe Harbor Framework (*http://export.gov/safeharbor/*).

tinues to play its influential role in privacy law, then a wise developer looking to build a product that might be used in the global private sector should keep an eye on the ongoing development of these new laws and design technology that could readily meet their requirements.

Meanwhile, the development of privacy laws affecting the government collection and use of data remains more uncertain. The fallout from the 2013 disclosure of pervasive surveillance by U.S. and other intelligence agencies continues, and it remains difficult to predict the ultimate outcome. Proposals have been submitted to governments around the world to modify the powers of government intelligence agencies to collect and use information, but few significant reforms have actually been enacted as of the publication of this book. While awareness of and concern over the exercise of government surveillance power is probably higher than it has been in decades,[10] that surveillance power remains relatively undiminished. Indeed, the dangers presented by the radicalization of extremists fighting in Syria and Iraq and the execution of bloody terrorist attacks such as those in Paris against the offices of the *Charlie Hebdo* magazine in early 2015 have generally lead to calls for increased government surveillance (*http://bit.ly/uk-internet-security*).

Consequently, some laws in the next 10 years might actually demand that developers *not* include certain capabilities that protect privacy because those capabilities might prevent government law enforcement and intelligence services from acquiring access to information they maintain could be vital to the detection and prevention of crime and terrorism. For example, following the aforementioned *Charlie Hebdo* incident, British Prime Minister David Cameron suggested the possibility of laws banning services that provide encrypted communication that cannot be read by security services, arguing that such services "allow safe spaces for (terrorists) to talk to each other."[11] On the other hand, such laws may also drive technology development in another direction, requiring developers to enhance privacy and security protections in order to defeat government access. For instance, following the revelations of U.S.-intelligence-led mass surveillance, some European authorities suggested that data could not be transferred to the U.S., as it was potentially not secure against government access.[12] Organizations that want to do business with Europe or other countries with similar concerns would therefore have to employ technology that would defeat any attempts at government intrusion.

---

10 See, e.g., a 2014 *USA Today*/Pew Research Center Poll (*http://bit.ly/usatoday-nsa-poll*) finding that 70% of Americans polled thought that they should not have to give up privacy in order to be safe from terrorism.

11 Trenholm, Rich. "British Prime Minister Targets Encrypted Messaging after Paris Attacks" (*http://bit.ly/cnet-encrypted*). CNET. January 12, 2015.

12 Essers, Loek. "European Data Concerns Cloud Outlook for US Vendors" (*http://bit.ly/eu-data-concerns*). Computerworld UK. September 19, 2011.

For a technology developer, all of this requires careful thought as to where to locate your business, where to locate your data, and where to sell your product. Those decisions will determine which of these frequently shifting laws apply to you and consequently will drive design decisions about the privacy capabilities that are incorporated into your product. Don't wait to hire a lawyer to advise you on these potential issues until after your product is built and ready to ship—legal advice at the design stage may save you substantial costs down the line if you are forced to redesign vast segments of your code base.

Greater Transparency and Control

Proposed legal reforms are often accompanied by calls for great transparency in data-collection and handling practices. Much of the concern over privacy stems not so much from the worry that someone *has* a person's data, but rather from the fact that a person does not know what is being *done* with that data. But just as technology has enhanced the ability for others to collect and analyze data about us, so too might it provide new opportunities for transparency *around* data processing and even help create greater individual control.

Two factors may drive an increase in data-processing transparency: one, a general increase in the amount of data available about those who collect and use information, and two, greater liability for misuse of data. The first stems from the dramatic increase in the amount of data available in the world. In addition to all of the information about individuals, there is also an increase in data *about* that data—or audit-log information (see Chapter 9), telecommunications metadata, financial transactional metadata, and so on. This "data about data" can create a detailed record of how information flows—who looked at what, when they looked at it, and what they did with it—creating a new level of potential accountability for data usage.

However, this depends in part on the ability of data subjects (or the individuals and organizations charged with oversight responsibilities) to get access to this data in order to review it. The second factor could come into play here. Increased liability for data misuse, such as the increased fines proposed in the aforementioned changes to the E.U. data protection regime, might create greater incentives not only for data owners to better monitor their own data handling practices but also to provide their "data about data" to data subjects (i.e., those to whom the data collected, stored, and used applies) as a means of demonstrating to those data subjects that their information has been handled responsibly.

Greater transparency in turn may lead to demands for greater control. Individuals who are more conscious of how their data is used might very well try to assert more control over those uses. Such control might involve requiring explicit consent for individualized data sharing decisions, as opposed to providing blanket consent for purpose-driven sharing at the time of collection. It might also involve allowing data subjects to review and correct information held about them, and asserting their "right to be forgotten" described above.

While some consumers have already expressed interest in exercising this level of control, large-scale adoption would mean millions of data subjects making countless particularized decisions about their data. The sheer size of data sets and the volume of sharing and usage decisions that might implicate just *one* person's data (let alone millions of people's data) presents an extremely complex technical and organizational challenge. But in the next decade, this hurdle may be overcome—either because law and policy will require it, or the next great innovator discovers a way to make it work effectively. If and when it happens, your data-management systems will need to incorporate these capabilities.

Privacy in Plain Sight

In general, information that is readily available can be collected about individuals by governments and private entities with minimal (if any) limitation, like taking a picture of a car on a public street. However, as data analysis becomes more sophisticated, the potential amount of information that might be derived from such seemingly innocuous data points is significant, including inferences of extensive personal information.[13]

However, a recent U.S. Supreme Court decision—*United States v. Jones*[14]—indicated that mainstream legal thought may be willing to extend the cloak of privacy to encompass some degree of public activity. The case involved the placement of a geo-locational tracking device on a vehicle for an extended period of time as part of an investigation into the activities of a drug dealer. Although the binding part of the Court Opinion ultimately turned on the physical trespass involved in placing the device on an individual's vehicle (therefore requiring a warrant issued under the Fourth Amendment), the assorted concurring opinions suggested more. These opinions read together indicated that there *may* be at least five votes willing to find that a warrant would have been required to observe the movements of a vehicle for an

---

13 The activities of a vehicle on a public street is information that can be collected, stored, and analyzed in most states without violating any privacy laws, as evidenced by the fact that both law enforcement (see, e.g., You Are Being Tracked (*http://bit.ly/aclu-tracked*)) and the private sector (see, e.g., Vigilant Solutions (*http://vigilantsolutions.com/*)) collect such information through the use of automated license plate reader (ALPR) systems. While an individual in a particular car might not be readily identifiable based on casual observation on the street, their identity may actually be discernible based on a surprisingly small number of data points. Furthermore, analysis of a more substantial set of data points concerning the movements of a car might allow the inference of an extensive amount of personal information about an individual, including religion, sexual orientation, health conditions or political affiliation, all based on a review of places the individual frequents such as churches, bars, clinics, and/or events.

14 132 S. Ct. 945 (2012)

extended period of time—even without physical trespass, and *even though all those movements occurred within plain view of any observer on public streets*. Justice Sotomayor wrote:

> "I would ask where people reasonably expect whether their movements will be recorded and aggregated in a manner that enables the government to ascertain, more or less at will, their political and religious beliefs, sexual habits, and so on... It may be necessary to reconsider the premise that an individual has no reasonable expectation of privacy in information voluntarily disclosed to third parties."

In short, Sotomayor and other Justices appear to be willing to consider a significant change in privacy law, recognizing that the collection and aggregation of publicly available information may reveal information that should have some degree of privacy protection.

This would mean there may soon be a legally recognized privacy interest in things that occur in public. Just as *Katz v. United States* moved privacy from the home to the person in 1967, so too may the progeny of *Jones* further modify the conception of a zone of privacy to beyond merely that which occurs outside of the view of others. Such a change would dramatically reshape the rules surrounding what data should be collected, stored, and processed. It would also significantly change how such data should be used, and when it can and cannot be shared with other parties. Such a finding could significantly alter your business model and the practices of any of your potential customers who might be using your product to interact with such information.

For example, both public and private organizations might no longer be able to freely collect social media information from publicly available social media sources. If such data is deemed to implicate a privacy interest, law and policy might be created that requires governments to obtain a warrant or pursue other legal avenues, or require private companies to obtain express consent from the individual data subject before they can collect and process this data. This data might also be subject to new handling restrictions, such as a requirement that those who collect this data must take reasonable measures to ensure that if the data is deleted from the social media platform, it's also deleted from any collecting organizations' data systems unless express consent is again obtained from the data subject allowing its retention.[15]

This is neither inherently positive nor negative. Rather, it means any company with a product built around the collection and use of public information should be prepared to respond with agility in the event of this potential shift in the privacy paradigm. Many of the technical solutions discussed in this book—or those as yet undreamt of

---

15 Note that this example only discusses social media usage limitations in the privacy context. Other limitations on such use—such as Terms of Service provisions—may apply to this data as well. In other words, ask your lawyer!

—could be applied to such products in response to these changes. Furthermore, companies that anticipate this potential change and enable privacy-protective collection in their current use of publicly available information could find themselves with a significant competitive advantage over those who wait to be pushed into such changes further down the road.

The Destiny of Data

In their book *Big Data*, authors Viktor Mayer-Schönberger and Kenneth Cukier describe the increasing *datafication* of our world.[16] Datafication refers to taking something that has never before been treated as data and turning it into a numerically quantified format. For example, they point to the work of Shigeomi Koshimizu, an assistant professor of mechanical engineering, involving the reading of pressure points of a person's posterior on a chair that allows researchers to identify individuals based on the unique way in which they sit. This research, they suggest, could be used as an anti-theft device in cars by being able to recognize when anyone but an approved driver is seated behind the wheel, or it could be used to identify changes in position that might indicate a driver has fallen asleep (thus triggering some sort of alarm to wake the driver).[17] Using this technology, something that was never quantified before—how one sits—is now quantified as a series of data points that can be added into the mix of "big data" analytics.

Datafication creates yet another surge of data generation in addition to the ongoing exponential growth of more traditional data sources (e.g., phone metadata, credit-card transactional data). A product designer will want to be cognizant of potential new data sources in order to capitalize on these sources as she iterates on her product over time. At the same time, the product designer will need to continually re-evaluate the potential privacy issues raised by these new data sources and be prepared to reconfigure the technical building blocks of privacy (or create new ones) to respond to novel ways in which new data sources may be collected and managed.

Product designers should also bear in mind the potential effects of their technology on existing data. Returning to social media, imagine a world in which Twitter information is collected ubiquitously by governments and private organizations. No single tweet goes uncollected and unanalyzed, and sophisticated algorithms are able to derive extremely detailed information about individuals that is subsequently utilized for highly targeted advertising, scientific research, voter engagement, and any number of other purposes. It is possible that the benefits of such usage might delight Twitter users. On the other hand, it is possible that such intense scrutiny might repulse

---

16 Mayer-Schönberger, Viktor, and Kenneth Cukier. *Big Data: A Revolution That Will Transform How We Live, Work, and Think*. London: John Murray, 2013. 15.

17 Ibid., 77.

users who do not find that the benefits of microblogging make up for the intrusion on individual privacy. Users then turn to some other means of communication and within a short timeframe the entire platform is abandoned or significantly diminished. The failure to exercise any self-control and to better respect or anticipate privacy interests might end up destroying the very data source that was the lifeblood of these business interests.

Anonymization Under Siege

While reports of the death of privacy are likely overstated, data anonymization is very much on life support. As discussed throughout the book, the bulk of privacy law hinges on identification; personal privacy is potentially infringed when dealing with information that can be directly linked to an individual. If no one knows who a data point is about, then there can be no violation of a person's privacy. Consequently, privacy law has generally given broad exemptions to the sharing of anonymized data. This traditionally has involved removing personally identifiable information, such as name or social security number, from a data set before sharing data, as shown in Figure 13-1.

In recent years, however, data scientists have taken advantage of the increasing availability of data and more powerful computers to test the resilience of basic anonymization techniques. Although removing the Name column from the spreadsheet in Figure A effectively obscures the identity of the individual data subjects for those only in possession of the spreadsheet, it does not account for the increasing ease of re-identification. A study by Latanya Sweeney—a leading privacy expert—revealed that 87% of the United States actually has a unique combination of birth date, gender, and zip code.[18] Someone in possession of those three data points (all frequently useful information that might be shared as part of an anonymized data set) might be able to re-identify people (whether in the role of patients, voters, or organization members) if they had the right set of identified data.

Further studies and experiments have continued to chip away at our confidence in the effectiveness of data anonymization, leaving many to conclude that the "anonymized" exception to data privacy laws and regulations should be reconsidered.[19] Data-protection regimes are already adapting to account for the existence of a spectrum of

---

18 Sweeney, Latanya. "Simple Demographics Often Identify People Uniquely" (*http://bit.ly/sweeney-simple-demo*). Carnegie Mellon University, Data Privacy Working Paper 3, 2000.

19 For an excellent discussion of these experiments and their potential effects on privacy law, see our Foreword author Paul Ohm's article, "Broken Promises of Privacy: Responding to the Surprising Failure of Anonymization" (*http://bit.ly/ohm-broken-promises*). As with all things in this space, there is a robust debate still underway. For an argument that perhaps de-identification is still viable, see Ann Cavoukian and Daniel Castro's "Big Data and Innovation, Setting the Record Straight: De-identification *Does* Work" (*http://bit.ly/pbd-deidentification*).

"identifiable" information sets—some more identifiable than others depending on the number of data points involved. These regimes operate under the principle that such information sets should also be subject to some (if not all) of the same privacy requirements as PII. While these changes may very well be important in ensuring that individual privacy is protected, inhibiting the flow of anonymized data may have negative effects on potentially beneficial data uses such as academic research and tracking health trends.

Name	Birth Date	Gender	Zip Code
John Doe	1/1/1990	M	00001
Jane Roe	2/2/1990	F	00002

Name	Birth Date	Gender	Zip Code
Person X	1/1/1990	M	00001
Person Y	2/2/1990	F	00002

Figure 13-1. A very basic anonymization scheme eliminates the identifying information —in this case, an individual's name.

Given the potential for a significant shift in how this data is regulated, product developers should be wary of basing their entire business on the analysis or sharing of anonymized data. At the same time, they should also see this as an opportunity to innovate and even save anonymization from its untimely death. Who knows what riches might await the developer who creates an anonymization engine that more effectively obfuscates data while retaining analytic utility? How big might the market be for a way to share anonymized data such that it cannot be easily integrated with other data sets, thereby preventing the application of computer-driven re-identification techniques? The possibilities are endless.

Expect the Unexpected

This is only a cursory skim of might happen in the world of privacy in the next decade. Just as Warren and Brandeis likely never could have conceived of an information-exchange vehicle like the Internet, we too are probably equally as blind as to what the world might bring in the next 100—or even 50, or 20—years.

On September 10, 2001, many people probably thought of the post-Cold-War world as an inherently safe place, focused more on increasing economic growth and less on domestic security concerns. A day later, the horrific attacks of September 11th sparked a significant change in global national security policies as governments shifted their concerns from identifiable nation-states largely playing by established rules to shadowy, nonstate, terrorist organizations unburdened by traditional international norms. When, where, and how nations gathered intelligence changed significantly, raising both traditional privacy concerns and surfacing entirely new concerns with the birth of novel surveillance techniques.

Events that will cause similar seismic shifts in societal norms and priorities are all but certain, but the form they will take is largely unknowable. A successful technologist is someone who uses foresight and creativity to anticipate what people need and want, and can provide those capabilities before anyone else. Applying this same foresight to anticipate and prepare for the unexpected in the privacy sphere will be a strong advantage to anyone wanting to make privacy an ongoing value-add for their business.

Yet even the most prescient engineer can't rely on vision alone, and over the course of this book, we hope we have provided a significant grounding in the basic toolkit of privacy engineering. We also hope you've reached the end of this book with a new appreciation for the importance of thinking about privacy as you design technology and a new understanding of some of the basic building blocks that might go into that design.

We have assiduously tried to avoid editorializing throughout this book. There are plenty of excellent books, articles, and papers out there engaging in a great debate on the merits or lack thereof of different approaches to privacy protection, and we encourage you to seek those out and to engage in what we believe is one of the most important discussions of our age. But we will indulge ourselves in these final paragraphs to offer one opinion that has driven the writing of this book.

When it comes to designing and building technology, there is no one more powerful than the engineer. Businesses depend on managers, investors, lawyers, accountants, salespeople, and any number of others to be truly successful, but at the end of the day it is the engineers who write the code and build the product. In doing so, they have the potential to change the world for the better—or for the worse. The products that they make in their cubicles, their garages, and their parents' basements can and do shift the decision landscape of the world. In a matter of months, a new technology can alter the fabric of human society—how we interact with our governments, businesses, and each other. An engineer needs to recognize what kind of society they might be creating with each line of code that they write. Then they must take that responsibility on their shoulders.

We believe that privacy is a necessity in our society. As Julie Cohen reminds us in the quote that opens this book, privacy is fundamental to a free society, to the defining of ourselves, and to the innovation that has marked almost the whole of human history. Yet it is a value that is consistently under threat, sometimes from those with malevolent plans and sometimes from those with the best of intentions. As engineers, we may be tempted to look for a modern Louis Brandeis who will rise up and defend privacy with passionate legal and philosophical arguments, and shoulder the burden of this crucial, complicated, and often thankless work. But in doing so, we would be shirking what also must be our own solemn duty.

The first line of defense in the fight to preserve privacy is you.

Index

About the Authors

Courtney Bowman has been working in the data analytics space for the last decade. He joined Palantir Technologies in 2010 as an in-house Privacy and Civil Liberties specialist. Within that role, he has developed extensive experience working with local and federal government agencies (including law enforcement, criminal justice, health, and social services) to develop technology-driven solutions to information sharing and interagency cooperation in a manner that respects applicable privacy, security, and data integrity requirements.

Ari Gesher is a technologist and software generalist who has split his career between systems engineering, software engineering, and writing and speaking about the uses and impacts of data analysis technologies. In his 17-year career, he's worked at a number of startups, was the maintainer of the SourceForge.net open source software repository before the word "GitHub" existed, and landed at Palantir as a very early engineer in 2006 (after dropping out of his undergrad education at the University of Illinois for a second time).

John K. Grant is a Civil Liberties Engineer at Palantir Technologies. He served for nearly a decade as an advisor in the U.S. Senate. He earned his law degree from Georgetown University shortly after joining the staff of the Senate Homeland Security and Governmental Affairs Committee.

Daniel Slate has worked at the nexus of privacy, technology, and security for the past six years. At one time a researcher for former cabinet-level national security officials, he has also worked as an engineering strategist and product manager for Palantir Technologies, where he focused on architecting privacy-safeguarding software for the international security community. He studied at Stanford University and splits his time between Northern California and Jerusalem.

Colophon

The animal on the cover of *The Architecture of Privacy* is a six-banded armadillo (*Euphractus sexcinctus*), also known as the yellow armadillo. Native to South America, this species inhabits the savannahs and grasslands of Argentina, Bolivia, Brazil, Paraguay, Suriname, and Uruguay. The word *armadillo* means "little armored one" in Spanish, a reference to the bony plates that protect the animal's head and body.

E. sexcinctus is typically yellow or reddish-brown in color, with a pointed head, short legs, and six to eight moveable bands between its armor plates. It is the second-largest armadillo species, measuring up 30 inches long and weighing about 15 pounds. A close relative of both the sloth and the anteater, it has sharp claws that make it adept at digging burrows.

The yellow armadillo is omnivorous, subsisting mostly on plant matter as well as insects. Due to its poor eyesight, it relies on its keen sense of smell to locate food. It is also diurnal, in contrast to most other armadillo species.

Many of the animals on O'Reilly covers are endangered; all of them are important to the world. To learn more about how you can help, go to *animals.oreilly.com*.

The cover image is from *Wood's Animate Creation*. The cover fonts are URW Typewriter and Guardian Sans. The text font is Adobe Minion Pro; the heading font is Adobe Myriad Condensed; and the code font is Dalton Maag's Ubuntu Mono.

Get even more for your money.

Join the O'Reilly Community, and register the O'Reilly books you own. It's free, and you'll get:

- $4.99 ebook upgrade offer
- 40% upgrade offer on O'Reilly print books
- Membership discounts on books and events
- Free lifetime updates to ebooks and videos
- Multiple ebook formats, DRM FREE
- Participation in the O'Reilly community
- Newsletters
- Account management
- 100% Satisfaction Guarantee

Signing up is easy:

1. Go to: oreilly.com/go/register
2. Create an O'Reilly login.
3. Provide your address.
4. Register your books.

Note: English-language books only

To order books online:
oreilly.com/store

For questions about products or an order:
orders@oreilly.com

To sign up to get topic-specific email announcements and/or news about upcoming books, conferences, special offers, and new technologies:
elists@oreilly.com

For technical questions about book content:
booktech@oreilly.com

To submit new book proposals to our editors:
proposals@oreilly.com

O'Reilly books are available in multiple DRM-free ebook formats. For more information:
oreilly.com/ebooks

CPSIA information can be obtained at www.ICGtesting.com
Printed in the USA
BVOW09s2237270915

419799BV00001B/1/P